I am profoundly moved. I am as sincere as I've ever been when I tell you that this book is absolutely one of the finest contributions to womankind that I have ever read. **It is superbly written,** *and I'm still feeling the spiritual, emotional connection to you and this incredible work. I am truly overwhelmed.* **I could not put this book down.**

—Dr. M. R. Roderiques, Psychotherapist

Wow! What a book! A real eye opener, *and I've never heard of down-low before. The book is very well written and planned out. It will connect immediately with the target audience in a way that few books do—and I have no doubts at all about that. I wish you great success with the sales of this book and that the purpose of it—that women will wake up and smell the coffee about the men they may be married to, and stick together as "sisters".*

—Ruth

Believe me when I say I could not sleep at all last night. The thoughts of what I read constantly went through my mind. After reading the section that described the types of advertisements and parties that down low 'men' participate in, I didn't know whether to cry, scream or just puke! believe this book will certainly enlighten others like me/us who had no real idea of this underground world. But, most importantly, **I hope that this will be a profound 'wake up call'** *for those sisters who are out there putting their trust, literally their lives in the hands of any good looking brother that comes their way, just to have a 'man'. Lack of education and action on our behalf is literally killing us! This was certainly eye opening for me!*

—Brenda

I love it, it's so real! It is awesome and tells it like it is and for those who will be ready to hear it for real will really like the book. The **Straight-Up Truth About the Down-Low** *gives an extreme amount of insight into what really goes on. People will be glad to read a book like that. It's heavy and for real.*
—Kim

Even though I knew what the book entailed, girls I must say this is a very informative book. **EVERY WOMAN NEEDS A COPY OF THIS!!!** *Doesn't matter what race, creed or color.*
—Natalie

The Straight-Up Truth About The Down-Low:

Women share their stories of betrayal, pain and survival

By Joy Marie

The Straight-Up Truth About The Down-Low:

Women share their stories of betrayal, pain and survival

By Joy Marie

Creative Wisdom Books
Manassas, Virginia

The Straight-Up Truth About The Down-Low:
Women share their stories of betrayal, pain and survival

By Joy Marie

Published by:
Creative Wisdom Books
P.O. Box 1154
Manassas, VA 20108
(703) 330-1996
CreativeWBooks@aol.com
www.straightuptruth.com

Quality Press, Project Coordinator / Consultant
The Printed Page, Interior Design / Cover Layout

The publication is designed to provide accurate and authoritative information in regard to the subject matter covered. It is sold with the understanding that the Publisher is not engaged in rendering legal, accounting or other professional services. If legal advice or other expert assistance is required, the services of a competent professional person should be sought.

CREATIVE WISDOM BOOKS are available at special discounts for bulk purchases, sales promotions, fund raising or educational purposes.

ISBN 978-0-9815443-2-8
Library of Congress Control Number: 2008922042

Dedication

This book is dedicated to all women. This is a wake up call reminding us to love, protect and value our hearts, our souls and especially our bodies.

Acknowledgments

Thank you, Heavenly Father for the guidance, the knowledge and the wisdom you have graced us with throughout our lives. We thank you that through our painful experience, you brought us together for a greater good. Thank you for helping us love ourselves again.

We are very grateful to and give special thanks to the courageous women who shared their stories with us. We thank you for putting a face on this crisis. The courage you demonstrated is remarkable and your stories have touched the hearts of many readers. You will always be very dear to us.

We would also like to thank you, Mrs. Yvonne Rose of Quality Press for sharing your professional wisdom with us and helping us turn our dream into a reality. Your warm and pleasant business style makes you a joy to work with.

We would also like to thank Ruth Blaikie for editing our book with such care. Your advice and encouragement was priceless.

Our heartfelt thanks are extended to our families and friends, for the love, patience and comfort you showed us through our ordeals. When we decided to write this book, you all believed in us. We could not have accomplished this without your support and encouragement. We will be forever grateful.

And on behalf of all women, a very special thank you to the brave men who shared their stories with virtual strangers. We hope other men will be inspired by you and thus be courageous and true to themselves and those they love.

Preface

The Purpose of This Book

Imagine…You have finally met Mr. Right. He's everything you dreamed of: handsome, sexy, charming, intelligent, articulate, and financially successful. He even portrays the role of an excellent father. He does not smoke, drink, or use drugs and he has a decent credit history. You marry him and buy your dream house in the suburbs. Your children attend the best schools and you live in a *wonderful* neighborhood. You're finally living the American dream—the perfect family—but one day you wake up and realize that your Prince Charming is really a lying Queen.

You can't believe it. It can't possibly be true. No, not him—and no, not you, but somewhere deep in your heart, you know it really is true. All the pieces of the puzzle were there, but you couldn't and didn't want to connect the dots because your heart refused to believe what your brain and your intuition were telling you. What happened to your dream, your life, and your sense of security? Something suddenly snatched it all away, but where were you? Why didn't you see it coming?

You discover your husband is secretly sleeping with men. He is part of the secretive subculture known as the "down-low." You feel shocked, disgusted, ashamed, humiliated, angry, stupid, foolish, victimized, hurt, betrayed, deceived, shattered, confused, devastated, and used. You feel dirty, violated, and terrified about the possibility of being infected with HIV or some other nasty STD. You find yourself on an emotional roller-coaster, riding high on denial and then plunging deep into despair, desperate to get off. You search frantically for answers; some sort of validation for your feelings and even something—anything—to prove you wrong. You surf the net desperately seeking information. However, you discover that the on-line support groups are geared toward helping the gay person come to terms with their own sexuality, but there's nothing to help you. You're left feeling ignored, overlooked, and victimized all over again.

You anxiously search the bookstores and libraries looking for any books on the subject. After reading the various books on the down-low, you are still left amazingly uninformed. You've read the book written by the gay man that actually faults the woman for one reason or another. When it comes to the black man, he even faults their culture. You've read "Mr. Down-low's" point of view that almost glorifies the lifestyle and makes it sound like an exclusive fraternity. You've also been given the account of "Mr. Down-low's" ex-wife who has forgiven and moved on 20 years after the experience. Although these books have been somewhat informative, they still have not touched on the real devastation left in the wake of this deceitful and cowardly lifestyle.

The purpose of this book is to provide support and resources for the wives, lovers, and families that have been victimized by homosexual men masquerading as straight. Our intent is to educate and inform women who may encounter men on the down-low and support the women who have experienced it already. We believe the account of our experiences and what we have learned will bring about awareness and a heightened sense of self-responsibility. There are plenty of people who only speak about this subject to defend the down-low, to further misinform women and/or to make money. We believe our lives should be in our own hands and not theirs. We have chosen to write this book in order to speak for ourselves and not allow someone else, who hasn't been through it, to tell our story.

This is not a book full of statistics, articles, or scientific data. It is written by two women who have experienced the anguish and misery of being married to men on the down-low. They share from the depths of their hearts, souls, and minds as they tell their own stories and the stories of other women who have lived through this devastating experience. Contrary to the beliefs of some authors, there *are* telltale signs when a man is on the down-low. We address those signs and answer many of your questions that have been ignored by other books written on the subject. Though the account of the down-low lifestyle is described in very graphic detail, we feel it is necessary to accurately portray the reality of this life-threatening behavior.

Contents

Introduction

What is the "Down-Low?"

The "down-low," "DL," "Tha Low," "Tha Low Low," all refer to men who secretly have sex with other men while in sexual relationships with women. She may be his wife, girlfriend, or just a friend with benefits, but the down-low specifies that she is not "in the know" about his homosexual activities. These men do not consider themselves gay or bisexual because they do not wish to be associated with gay, effeminate men. In fact, they actually shun all labels. Some of them consider their secretive homosexual lifestyle to be just another extracurricular activity. Although the term "down-low" originated in the African-American community to indicate something on the "hush-hush," it is now used to describe men of all races who have sex with other men undercover. We have found that this behavior is not new, nor is it specific to black men who have sex with men. White men who engage in this same dangerous behavior are said to be "in the closet."

From our research, we have discovered there is really no difference between Black men being on the down-low and any other men being in the closet—they are *all* closeted homosexuals. These men come in all ages, races, shapes, sizes, professions, and even religions. Most are hard to detect at first glance. Some of these men have been practicing this lifestyle for many years and therefore have become very skillful at hiding their true identities.

They believe that what they do privately is their own business and what we don't know won't hurt us.

On the contrary, this lifestyle is very much our business. We, as women who love, trust, and share our lives with men, deserve to know if they are engaging in risky, dangerous, and potentially murderous sexual activities. We have the right to be able to make informed choices for our own lives. Although there has been no definitive research published linking men on the down-low as a cause of the HIV/AIDS epidemic in African-American women, it does not take a rocket scientist to link the two. Our purpose is not to engage in debate about whether or not the down-low is a contributory factor in the rise of HIV/AIDS rates in Black women. Our intent is to make women aware of the dangerous, promiscuous sexual practices that actually take place in this lifestyle.

The ways in which these men "hook up" prove that most often they are having sex with strangers. There is no way for them to know if that person is infected with HIV or another STD. There are also men who have long-standing down-low relationships, oftentimes with so-called best friends, right under their wives' noses.

Our research indicates that most down-low networking is done on the Internet. Many of the Internet sites are free and only require a password, profile, and maybe a photograph. The following profiles were taken from actual web sites of down-low men seeking sexual encounters. Some of these excerpts are extremely graphic; however, we want women to realize that these same men are going home, after these encounters, to sleep with their wives and girlfriends. These profiles were randomly chosen from personal ads created by down-low men and not by men who are openly gay.

> MascDL 36, 5'11" 175 lb, 33 waist, athletic build, bald head, smooth, black, Looking for 1-on-1 sex.

"Don't get it twisted. I still love fuckin pussy and I take care of home, just lookin for a bruh who is masculine about his shyt, DL, tight body that can handle this ass, then flip over and take this dik!! Married and bi bruhs step to the front of the line."

More info about MascDL:

Casual, **NOT OUT**, doesn't smoke, drinks occasionally, doesn't use drugs, Zodiac Scorpio. Versatile, (meaning top or bottom) 9.5" (the size of his penis), Cut (circumcised), Safe sex only, HIV- (meaning negative) Prefers meeting at your place.

Hobbies: The gym, traveling, Fuckin.

BiBlkDlBtm 28, 5'6",160 lb 26 waist, athletic build, shaved hair, some body hair, black, Looking for 1-on-1 sex, 3some/Group sex, Misc fetishes

"Sup Brothas? Bi DL bottom bro from San Antonio, TX in town for the week on business looking to hook up with kewl big dik tops for sexual pleasure and fun. No games please. You won't be disappointed so hit me up.

More info on BiBlKDlBtm:

Conservative, **NOT OUT**, doesn't smoke, drinks occasionally, doesn't use drugs, Zodiac Cancer.

11-inch Bone, 29, 6'0, 30 waist, Athletic Build, Black hair, Smooth, Mix, Looking for Misc Fetishes

Be a blk top man…. I give up head/Azz wit serious skillz!!! Definitely private and discrete. Damn, what you think

secret lover for you means. "*Best kept secret of married, bi, curious, high-profile and xdl blk SGL men!!! Makin u bust!!....marinate....ahhhhhhhh. Nutt'n bounce.*

OUT NO. 9" cut, Ph.D satisfying bros on the dl.

38, 6'3", 194lb, 33w Athletic, Black, Some Body Hair, Black , Looking for Friendship, Relationship, 1-on-1 Sex

I luv phonebone! I luv the REAL THING 2. I need a man 2 cater 2 me. Passionate! Intimate! Ambitious! Artistic! Determined! What I do cums from the heart. U do U. I do me. Let's share & LIVE life together. 2 soak N your warmth! It takes 1 awesome bro 2 KEEP my puzzy wet. Where r u?

Where is that brotha that will cater to my needs? Where is that brotha that wants to take it slow?

Casual, **OUT NO**, Smoke No, Drink Socially, Drugs No, Zodiac Aries, Bottom, 9" Uncut, **HIV POSITIVE**, prefer meeting at: Your Place.

If no face Pic in your Ad Don't bother to hit!!!!!

Looking for masculine bruthas who are into late night or early morning kinky phone sex. Holla. I'm looking for only masculine bros who N 2 hardcore kinky phone sex str8 up meaning bros who want to be pissed on, shitted on, spanked, paddled, fisted, footed, handcuffed, caged, degraded, gang banged, and nipple play. Only true filthy, masculine, hardcore smutdawgs?? My interests include water sports, ass play, nipple play, spitting, sniffing/licking pits, FEET, dil

Jock, **NOT OUT,** doesn't smoke, drinks occasionally, doesn't use drugs, Zodiac Libra.

Top, 11", Cut, Anything goes, HIV negative, will meet anywhere. Barbershop owner.

2007-02-15, 4:10 PM CST

I'm a young str8 business MAN by day but tonight I want to be someone's bitch. I wanna be fucked, not just in a bed but against the wall, bent over…whatever, as rough as you can give it. My stats are 22yo, black boy, 5'7, 150#, thin waist, round ass, 9in cut and a total btm. You have to send a pic and I'll send mine. I want a good pounding by someone somewhat near my age. I can host tonight, or tomorrow, or if you get to me before 4:45, I'll cum to you. My place or yours, whatever let's fuck. Send stats and a pic.

This is in or around Atlanta

If you are not serious dont waste ur time to hit me up.

I AM LOOKING FOR THEM FREAKY DOMINATE TOPS MEN.. LOVE THEM MANSS WITH THEM SMEELLLYY BALLS THAT WANNA RUB THEM ALL IN MY FACE..I WANT A MAN WITH THEM SWEATY BALLS THAT WANT ME TO SUCK IT AND LICK AND SUCK THEIR DICK. I WANNA GET REAL NASTY I WANT SUM ONE TO FUCK MY FACE NUTT ALL ON ME PISS ON ME. THEM FREAKY MANSS THAT LIKE IT KINKY AND NASTY HIT ME

UP IF U HAVE ANY OTHER IDEAS ABOUT WHAT U WANNA DO. I WANT TO DO WHATEVER NASTYY THINGGS U WANNA DO. LOVE THEM SMELLY BALLSS:)

More info on the above:

Jock, **NOT OUT**, doesn't smoke, drinks occasionally, doesn't use drugs, Zodiac: Pisces.

This is in or around St. Louis

—————————————————————————

MrBigDik4U

32, 5'9", 175 lbs, 33 waist, Athletic build, Black Hair, Some body hair, black, Looking for relationship, 1-on-1 sex, 3some/Group sex

Long lasting black top looking for bottoms who can take an intense ass pounding, not looking for virgins or those guys who complain "it hurts" right when you put it in. I like to eat a clean ass, suck big dik and deep fuck some butt hole, also love to have may ass eaten and dik sucked. Hairy guys to the front of the line, can't host.

More info on MrBigDik4U:

NOT OUT, doesn't smoke, drinks socially, doesn't use drugs, Zodiac: Sagittarius. Top, 8.5", Cut, Anything goes, HIV negative, prefer meeting at your place.

This is in and around Chicago.

—————————————————————————

IFUCKRAW

No condoms allowed!!!

27, 5'10" 190 lb, 34 waist, average build, black hair, smooth, black, looking for 1-on-1 sex, 3some/Group sex

Not trying to make any friends. If it happens so be it, real sexy bro here who loves to freak raw (meaning without condom). I want to feel that warm nutt deep in my hole and I want to cum deep in you. Completely versatile, but tops and bottoms welcome. Big dik tops first preference. Smokers a plus.

More about IFUCKRAW:

Casual, **NOT OUT**, smokes, drinks occasionally, doesn't use drugs. Versatile, 9.5", Cut, Anything goes, **HIV-POSITIVE**, Prefer meeting anywhere. Taking raw dik, want to get double-teamed by two big diks. Work Monday thru Friday

---

9miles4U, 23, 5'10", 260 lb, 40w, Large build, Black hair, some body hair, looking for relationship.

This is what I am looking for. A cool dude that I can hit the STR8 clubs, play Xbox, PS2 and gamecube wit, hang on a regular, workout wit, maybe hit up on a couple of females with and do the damn thang. Get down with each other sometimes. A BEST FRIEND I can do everything with. Be dawgs. Be around my age. Don't be into the 'GAY" lifestyle. Be a man. A dude that is not out to his family and closest friends. I want a closet dude like me. MEANING NOT OUT

More on 9miles4U:

> **NOT OUT,** doesn't smoke, drinks occasionally. Top, 9",
> Cut, Safe Sex Only, HIV negative, prefer meeting at your
> place.

> hotazz, 32, 5'9", 155 pounds, 30 waist, slim build, black
> hair, smooth, black, looking for 1-on-1 sex,
> 3some/Group sex.
>
> *Sup Fellas? Kewl brotha here, looking to get wit quality
> and solid people that are not full of that BROWN STUFF.
> I love to get this ass smashed, and eatin out real good, (ass
> eaters are a plus).*

More on hotazz:

> Conservative, **NOT OUT,** Don't smoke, doesn't drink,
> doesn't use drugs, Scorpio. Oral, 7.5", Cut, prefer meet-
> ing anywhere.

> Date: 2007-03-26, 5:33PM EST
>
> **Wife's at work** and looking to drop to my knees for a
> verbal d/d (disease and drug) free masc. man who likes
> his dick worshipped. Face fuck me, cum all over my
> face—and if you can do it again, cum on top of the first
> load. Hit me up with pic.

This is in or around Atlanta

Date: 2007-03-29, 9:37AM EST

Total bottom here, love to get fucked hard and suck a dick deep down my throat. Looking to see if I can get a GB going at my hotel room, with me being the only bottom. Or see how many dudes want to come by and dump a load. Use my mouth and ass for a cum dump, Kink is cool as well. Please have a pic. Cum in me Baltimore. I am a d/l black male, 30, 5'8, 145lbs, black hair, brown eyes, smooth body (shaved body). I will be visiting Baltimore next week for work and would love to see how much Baltimore cum I can get.

In and around downtown Baltimore.

Here are some of the actual screen names used by down-low men seeking men for encounters that were found on a very popular web site:

FuqMyBlkAzz	Gimmiedatassboyee	Goodbooty
DropnbigDCdik	8inch2suk	DeepInsideYou
Dik2ride	DLPython	DCFreakyRedBone
DatSexyChocNigg	Chocjock	Brothzkeepa
Bmorefreakin	BowleggedBrotha	BoiGotSkillz
Blkmusclebttm	Blkrawsex	Blksxy69
BlkBgDik	BlkItalianFrk	BlkBeef8
Addictive69	All4U	DLballer
1DLbruh	1SexyThug	BareNecessity
SlangNdathang	Redy2fk	PipeKid
PackinAlotOMeat	Oraltopnigga	Ondalow2003
Tapdisazz	CumwetmyDik	StickNitnu
Salad4U	Hungpoet	Tightnsweet
Ucumicum5	Dmagicstik	Thisazzis4U
ButtaNut	UpinMe	WetnHard
AltdikRider	Blkbootylover	HarryHole
Lettmesukit	DCGooddikk	Nuttuppinme

These are a few of thousands of profiles and solicitations posted by down-low men that were found on the Internet. There are thousands of such profiles listed in major U.S. cities, such as Washington DC, Atlanta, Baltimore, Chicago, New York City, Houston, Los Angeles, Seattle, and Charlotte, just to name a few. Ladies, be aware that most of these profiles contain pictures depicting gorgeous men and we mean absolutely gorgeous, fine-looking men who look straight. Some list their occupations as engineers, lawyers, business owners, and even doctors. Most are married or in heterosexual relationships and as you read above, are **NOT OUT** meaning **not out of the closet**... they are on the down-low. They have posted pictures of their erect penises, spread butt cheeks, and anuses. Some of these pictures (pics as they call them), show them in various sexual poses with other men, with semen on their faces and anuses, wearing thongs, engaged in group sex, holding their penises, giving blow jobs with their faces blacked out, shower scenes, sex in the woods and using many different hotel rooms.

Down-low men also deliberately seek out anonymous sex with other men in places such as adult bookstores, public restrooms, highway rest areas, parks, gyms, and bathhouses. Adult bookstores often have back rooms with private video booths that not only allow for private masturbation, but also have what are known as "glory holes." A glory hole is a small fist-sized hole between the video booths that is placed about hip-high for a man to place his penis through to let the stranger on the other side perform on him whatever sexual act he pleases. Both anal and oral sex is commonly practiced through glory holes. These glory holes are also found in men's public bathroom stalls. Public bathrooms friendly to this type of activity are often called "Tearooms." These practices are so common that all a man has to do is enter the restroom stall and wait for another man to enter the stall next to him. The hook-up ritual begins with one man tapping his foot multiple times, which is the universal gay code for wanting public sex. If the other man is interested, he will tap his foot in a similar manner. This will go back and forth a few times to make sure it is not a mistake. The men will begin to move their feet closer to each other. From that point, a hook-up is made either to have sex there in the bathroom or plans are made to go elsewhere. Sex is also performed out in the open in such places as public parks after hours and even during lunch hours in the back seat of a car. On the Internet, one man posted his park experience as follows:

> *"This place is unbelievable. I got fucked by six men in four hours. You can do anything here, blow jobs, full sex, jack-off parties, you name it."*

Other places where men can have multiple sex partners are at group sex parties, often called "DL" parties. Some of the men even wear hoods and masks to hide their identities from each other. Two such DL parties were advertised as follows:

Party4Tops&Bttms

> *"A few bruhs chilling this Sunday—chill ou— freak ou— smoke and whatever, must be masculine and athletic to muscular. Bottoms must be able to take a dik like we say take a dik. Your pic will be required in order to get on the invite list."*

Partyatthehouse

> *"Anything goes… open all night for only $20… upstairs/ downstairs, 5 bedrooms, pornos, food, mucho alcohol, cumm fuk all night… remove clothes at the door."*

Other locations that down-low men meet are places that everyone frequents on a regular basis in their everyday lives, such as hardware type stores, supermarkets, gas stations, on the job and even in churches. Popular gay cruise spots include hardware and electronic stores, department store and mall restrooms, fast-food restaurants, and mainstream bookstores. Knowledge of the activities that really go on in many men's restrooms should automatically bring about a safety concern for parents of young boys.

Bathhouses, which were very popular prior to the HIV explosion, are still convenient locations for down-low men to engage in anonymous sex. According to Wikipedia, a gay bathhouse is a sauna or steam bath where men go to have sex with other men. Wikipedia also stated that bathhouses are still used by men who do not identify as gay or bisexual, but who have sex with men, as well as by those who are closeted and/or in heterosexual relationships and by some men who identify primarily as heterosexual. Bathhouses are not as popular today as they once were; however the local gym has filled that void these days. The local gym is one of the favorite hook-up spots for down-low men, with homosexual activity taking place between jocks, muscle builders, personal trainers and male aerobic instructors. In other words, some men that look totally masculine and carry themselves as supremely macho are using their local gym as the primary site to find new male sexual partners as well as to engage in group sex.

We have given this graphic picture of what we have discovered because we want you to understand what really takes place in this down-low culture. These men are not just having love affairs, falling in love with other men by happenstance, but are actively seeking sex in all the ways you read above in their profiles and more. These same men are coming home to their wives and girlfriends, engaging in sex with them, kissing them on their lips, kissing their innocent children, most times before even showering. Some down-low men often feel dirty and disgusted with themselves after engaging in these homosexual liaisons and many times come home and immediately have sex with their wives or girlfriends in order to feel like a man again. Other down-low men immediately have sex with their wives to give the women a false sense of security by making them think they are the only one.

Ladies, let's be real. The down-low man does unseemly things with his mouth and other body parts with virtual strangers that he "hooks up" with on the streets, the Internet, the gym, cruise strips, etc. These sexual practices include anal sex, oral sex, "rimming" (licking the anus), and multiple sex partners at one time. Many of them engage in anal sex without a condom, which they refer to as "barebacking" or "raw."

Anal sex is the riskiest form of sexual activity when it comes to the transmission of HIV/AIDS. Tiny tears in the anal tissue, caused by the penetration of the penis, act as superhighways for the HIV virus, giving them access to the body through the blood stream. Anal tears provide an opening for all the other STDs as well. The man that penetrates the anus with his penis (referred to as a top) is also at risk because HIV can enter his blood stream through the tip of his penis or through small cuts, abrasions, or open sores. Even using condoms is not safe because condoms are more likely to break during anal sex than during vaginal sex. A number of studies have also indicated that oral sex can result in the transmission of HIV and other STDs.

"Rimming," also known as salad tossing, is the act of performing oral sex on the anus. Some of the diseases these men can be exposed to while "eating ass" (as they call it), is HIV, hepatitis A, intestinal parasites, bacterial infections, and other STDs, such as gonorrhea of the throat. These diseases are spread through oral contact with the blood, semen, and fecal matter of an infected person. As you read in the profiles above, many down-low men engage in the act of "rimming," as well as oral sex. Some down-low men only engage in oral sex (blow jobs). Some actually believe the falsehood that only the act of penetration makes a person gay. These men are of course in deep denial, lying to themselves as well as to their wives and girl-friends about their sexual orientation.

Ladies, we face a dangerous situation when our partners deceive us into assuming they are straight when they are really gay. We are not trashcans, but human beings that have the right to make informed decisions for our own lives—the operative word being "informed." We are not bashing men or generalizing that all men are on the down-low. There has been what seems to be a line of defense drawn by some African-American men who say it's all a conspiracy to further vilify the Black man. There are those who say it's just another way to further divide the Black man/woman relationship. Others have dubbed the down-low as nothing more than sensationalism designed to scare all women away from Black men. Through our research we have found that down-low behavior is not exclusive to Black men, therefore making the "vilify the Black man" statement just another smokescreen to divert attention and concern. This smokescreen is used to give women a false sense of security by telling them "don't believe the hype;" "it's not as widespread as people say;" or "it's only the fad of the moment." They also want you to believe that the existence of the down-low is only a myth.

The media has even portrayed the down-low lifestyle in a pristine, even sympathetic way, sometimes utilizing illustrations depicting one man holding another in a loving embrace. We suspect that this is being done to pacify the gay community. Ladies, we want you to really "get it." Even if two men on the down-low are in love, the sexual activities they practice, as discussed above, are dangerous and life threatening to you. We are not homophobic, but choose to identify that it's the deception of the down-low way of life that is taking its toll on our lives.

Part One

The Women Share Their Pain

Husbands, love your wives, just as Christ loved the church and gave himself up for her to make her holy, cleansing her by the washing with water through the word, and to present her to himself as a radiant church, without stain or wrinkle or any other blemish, but holy and blameless. In this same way, husbands ought to love their wives as their own bodies. He who loves his wife loves himself. After all, no one ever hated his own body, but he feeds and cares for it, just as Christ does the church for we are members of his body. For this reason a man will leave his father and mother and be united to his wife, and the two will become one flesh.

—Ephesians 5:25–31 (NIV Life Application Bible).

"My Fairy Tale"

Janine & Gary

I grew up in a quiet working class neighborhood of South Central Los Angeles before the influx of the recent gang activity. I was the shy middle child of six children with both my parents living at home. My childhood was basically uneventful. What we lacked in money, my parents made up for with plenty of love. I had many friends and I was a good student in school, maintaining mostly As and Bs in my college prep courses.

I met Gary during my junior year in high school. I went to a party with my friends, which I later found out was given by Gary's cousin, Stanley. I went into the kitchen for a drink and there was this tall, funny-looking guy serving the punch. He started cracking jokes and had me laughing for the rest of the evening. Toward the end of the party, he finally asked me to dance and we slow danced to Cameo's *Why Have I Lost You*. He whispered to me that I felt good in his arms. I could hear those words for years and years after they were spoken. Before we left the party, he asked me for my phone number and I gave it to him. About one week later, he called me and we talked on the phone for hours about any and everything. I knew in my heart that I could grow to love this guy. We started hanging out and from that point were inseparable. We fell deeply in love. As we shared the next few months together, we trusted each other with our most intimate secrets. I learned that he had lived through a very traumatic childhood, which endeared him to me even more. He spent the next couple of years practically living at my house and my entire family embraced and loved him also. I loved him so much and knew that he loved me, so near the second year of our court-ship, we made love, which was the first time for both of us. I didn't know what it meant for other girls to give their virginity away, but I knew what it meant for me. He would be my real, only true love. It was settled.

We loved being together. He was so funny and we laughed all the time. He wrote poetry and would read it to me on romantic picnics. We went on long Sunday drives and talked about our dreams and our future together. We would ride along the coastline of Palos Verdes, making plans to marry at the famous glass church that overlooked the beautiful shores of the Pacific Ocean. He would tell me over and over how happy I would be as his wife. We would have two children and he would buy me a beautiful home in the suburbs. I was still that shy young girl, but around him I came to life. I was a princess… and he was my prince.

After two years of being inseparable, everyone knew we were an item. One summer evening, after our high school prom and graduation were behind us, Gary came over as usual. We snuck out back to our favorite spot, in the back of my mom's old car and made love. We talked and kissed for a while and as he held me I realized that something was different. Gary seemed very upset and nervous. I looked at him and asked him what was wrong. With tears in his eyes and a trembling voice he told me he had joined the Marine Corps in order to get away from his family and therefore had to leave me behind, but just for a little while. My heart felt like it broke into a million pieces. After allowing myself to feel the initial shock and heartache, I decided to listen to Gary and try to understand why he was leaving me. He explained to me that he had nothing to offer and that I was his princess and he wanted to give me the best.

He wrote this farewell inscription to me in my high school yearbook.

> *"To the person I care the most about. Baby, I hope I will always be your number one because you are my number one. I will be happy when I can be a better man for you because I think you should have the best so that is what I want to be to you.*
>
> *Janine, I love you, more than anything in the whole wide world. I say to myself every day that I am so lucky to have a lady as good, kind, sweet, loving, and beautiful as you.*
>
> *Babe, I will be gone for a little while and I am going to pray to God every night and ask him to keep an eye on you and take care of you for me. I am going to ask him to give you back to me.*
>
> *Baby, I love you and always will,*
>
> *Love*
>
> *Gary"*

I went on to college as planned, while he did his tour in the marines. We wrote faithfully in the beginning and kept our flame alive for many, many months. We had every intention of being together again. After boot camp, he was actually stationed near home so we could see each other and our relationship grew stronger. However, Uncle Sam had other plans and soon he was sent 3000 miles away. We still kept in contact for a few months, but then, as often happens with long-distance relationships, we began to drift apart and finally all communication stopped. We went on with our lives and eventually married other people. I had two children and he had a daughter.

Twenty-five years later, imagine my surprise when I went on the Internet one day and discovered an e-mail from Gary. The e-mail read, "Tweety, this is me, Poo Bear." These were our nicknames for each other. He had found me through Classmates.com. I was so happy and surprised. I screamed with delight and instantly responded to his e-mail with my telephone number and told him to call me immediately! Later that evening, I heard the voice of my first love, a man I had never forgotten. Like a replay from the past, we talked for hours. It was like we were never apart. We shared that we were both separated from our spouses and how it must have been fate, or even God, because we had found each other at the time our hearts needed love the most.

We continued to talk by phone over the next year. Gary lived on the east coast and I still lived in California. One year later, Gary called and told me he was flying to California the next day. I was PMS-ing and was feeling bloated, fat, and unattractive and not in the mood for company. We met the next evening at a Karaoke bar where we were having a birthday party for my sister. When I saw him, I came alive again. I no longer felt bloated, fat, and unattractive, because I was the princess again, young and beautiful. All the warm memories flooded my mind and I was close to tears. It couldn't be him. That skinny, funny-looking guy that made me laugh had truly become a prince for real. He was so fine—tall and handsome with big brown smoldering, sultry, bedroom eyes. Oh my God!!!! Thank you, Jesus. He smiled at me and our eyes told the story of our love so long ago. He stood up and stretched out his arms and I jumped into them, wrapping my legs around his waist. I was home.

We continued to enjoy the party that night. He sang and brought the house down. When the party ended, he held me like he never wanted to let me go. The next day when he left for home, I knew this was not the end of the story. While he was still in the air, I called him and left a message on his cell. I told him that before I was 45, I would be his wife. That same evening, my mom called and during our conversation she told me that Gary had called her and said "I am still in love with your daughter." She said he was so excited, almost child-like again when he stated "Mom, Mom, it's like we never parted. It's like we have been together all of these years." My heart fluttered when my mom repeated his words to me.

For the next year we talked on the phone every day. Every time the phone rang my heart would jump with anticipation, because I knew that for the next few hours he would make love to me on the phone. He stroked and caressed me with his words. When he sang to me, I felt like I was the most beautiful woman in the world. His voice, full of promises, teased and drew me in. He comforted my mind with soothing reassurance. I was falling so hard. It was like an avalanche now—completely unstoppable. Before I knew it I had given all my heart, my mind, everything, to this man, the man I thought I would never see again, but the man I could never forget. I crossed thresholds with my thoughts of intention like I had never done before. I was reckless, adventurous, spontaneous, and excited all over. My whole body tingled whenever I thought of him.

Gary and I flew back and forth to see each other and cried every time we parted. Those big bedroom eyes made me feel like the most desired woman on earth. He said, "Tweety, I feel like I can't breathe when we're apart." As parting became more and more difficult, we began to make plans to be together forever just like we said we would when we were young.

Within a year of reuniting with Gary, we discussed our plans and decided it would be easier for me to transfer my job to the east coast. I sold my house, the very first home I had ever acquired by myself. I was so proud of it. I sold all my furniture and even some of my sentimental mementos in order to lighten the load and begin our new life. I transferred my job and Gary flew to California and drove me and my son to our new home on the east coast. My daughter had already gone away to college. We moved into an apartment temporarily, while our dream home was being built from the ground up. Together we chose every amenity and detail in our new home, from the cherry hardwood floors on the first level to the romantic three-sided fireplace in our master bedroom. Gary actually proposed to me on the newly poured foundation of our dream home. I cried as he read his yearbook inscription to me in the presence of our three children. I was so happy. Our lives seemed perfect. Eight months later, we received the keys to our new home. We were married the same evening in our empty dining room. We were ready to start our lives together as husband and wife.

For a while, my life seemed perfect. I had a handsome husband, a brand new home, we both had stable careers and our children were happy and secure. My husband went to work every day and came home on time every night, which gave me such a sense of security. He gave me total control over our money since he felt I was better able to handle the finances. I should have been a very happy woman, but for some reason, I wasn't. I started spiraling into a deep depression and I could not understand why. I had always been a high functioning woman, able to handle 50 things at one time, and here I was unable to get out of bed. I didn't know what was wrong with me. I thought I was cracking up inside. Little did I know my dream would quickly become a nightmare.

Looking back, I have always had some type of uncertainty about my husband. He seemed too good to be true. Before moving to be with him, I had seen the episode on Oprah, featuring J. L. King about Black men on the down-low and the show really bothered me. Although my husband is very masculine, he had a few effeminate quirks that showed up every blue moon in his mannerisms, and then sometimes he had a strange lilt to his voice. I talked to my very best friend about it and she said, "Well, you know, he did grow up in a house full of women, so you really have nothing to be concerned about." Later that evening, I asked Gary if he was gay or bisexual and if he had ever slept with a man. I even asked him if he was attracted to men. He told me that he thought a man sleeping with a man was disgusting and he would never do such a thing. Something else that bothered me was that Gary would often shave his chest and pubic hair even after I told him it was a turn-off to me.

About four months into our marriage, I noticed that Gary was very secretive about certain aspects of his life. For example, sometimes he would just suddenly appear dressed and at the door and all he would say was, "I'll be right back." It would be three to four hours or more before he came home. He also seemed overly cautious with his cell phone, keeping it close to him at all times and would get upset if I answered it. I didn't understand this because I opened all of our mail and I thought I was privy to every aspect of his life, as he was to mine. After all, he *was* my husband and I had no secrets from him. He was always on his cell phone and the majority of the phone calls were on his way to and from work. I became very suspicious and began to go over our cell phone bill with a fine-tooth comb, but I could never find anything. I would watch him leave for work in the morning and as I stood in the window to wave goodbye or just watch my handsome husband drive away, he never knew I was even watching him, because as he drove out of the garage, the cell phone was already up to his ear.

My husband always had a lot of acquaintances, but never had any close male friends. I found myself getting jealous when he would run off to chat with the male neighbors and I couldn't understand why I was feeling this way. I felt myself acting possessive and catty around certain men, and I didn't know why as it wasn't my usual nature. It was an uncomfortable feeling that had me bewildered. Our conversations began to become very boring and he seemed so uninterested in anything I had to say.

Our sex life, although very physically satisfying, was very emotionally unfulfilling for me because there was no intimacy. The deep love and passion we shared before was no longer there. I realize that love changes; however, this was different. His performance in bed was almost mechanical. The way he used to gaze into my eyes, which melted my heart and soul, was gone. I also noticed that I could walk around our beautiful bedroom with nothing on and my husband's eyes would not leave the TV. I could take a steamy shower with him and he would not get an erection. I would try to squeeze up against him in bed at night and he would nudge me away. Here I was, a newlywed, married only a few months, yet I felt very lonely and insecure. He said he would make me happy. He said he went away to the Marine Corps so he could become a better man for *me*. He had asked God to give me back to him and I thought his prayer had been answered. He told me that from the time he first left me, a piece of his heart was missing and now because he had me back in his life, he felt whole again. What was happening?

One night, around midnight, I was lying in bed feeling extremely sad and lonely. I had been crying all day. My husband was sound asleep beside me. Something told me to listen to Gary's cell phone messages. I lay there for a while and contemplated what to do because I didn't want to violate his privacy. The voice became louder and told me to check his cell phone. I slid out of bed and took Gary's cell phone from his night table. I took it into the bathroom and listened to his messages from our children as well as other usual mundane messages. My hands were already shaking, it was almost as if I knew something disturbing was about to happen. Suddenly, I heard a man's voice calling my husband, "Baby." My heart started pounding, I couldn't breathe, and my body began to tremble from head to toe. The man was telling him how good he looked as he walked into the office today. He called him "his baby," and sounded very proud. As I was reeling from shock, I heard another voice message from the same man, telling Gary he couldn't get together with him at the job this weekend and he hoped he wasn't mad. He also said, "The lifestyle is very difficult and he only wanted one thing." He then said, "Baby, you really put something on my mind and I can't stop thinking about it." The tone was very intimate like a man would speak to his woman. I was in total shock, but what was really strange is I felt the depression lifting from my body. I now knew the source of it.

For the first few minutes, I walked around in a blurry haze, shocked and scared. I knew my life was about to change from the dream life we had built together. It was so surreal. I felt total despair. In a dream-like state, I walked over to his side of the bed and looked down at him in utter disbelief. Who was this man? How could he have deceived me this way? I knew that I had to face the truth now. I reached down and shook him out of his peaceful slumber and as usual he looked up at me with a little smile.

"Yes, Baby?" he said.

I just screamed, "How could you? How could you do this to me?!!!"

"What's wrong?" he asked with a confused look on his face.

"I listened to your cell phone messages."

His eyes got big and I saw the fear that instantly jumped out of them.

"You're going to try to destroy me."

I kept screaming and shouted, "I asked you if you slept with men before I moved out here and you lied to me and told me, 'no.' I came three thousand fuckin' miles for *this*…how could you? You said you loved me."

"I thought we were friends, Gary; I thought I could trust you."

"You lying bastard! How could you?" and then I asked him, "Who is this man?"

"I'm not telling you," he calmly replied.

He sat up in bed, silent, with his eyes turned away from me as I stood there frozen in agony and terror with tears streaming down my face. Because he wouldn't look at me or answer any of the questions I hurled at him, I stormed out of the room and went down to the family room and lay on the couch. I cried all night long. I felt completely helpless. At first, I couldn't get my mind to wrap around the truth. This wonderful, gorgeous man, who I loved so much, had lied to me, tricked me, deceived me, conned me, and played with my emotions. The visions that started to flood my mind of him and another man were so disgusting and vile to me that I couldn't believe it. He was actually on the down-low. My husband sleeps with men. I wanted to die.

The next few days were a complete blurry haze. I was zombie-like. I had awakened that morning with a splitting headache from crying all night. I walked around my beautiful home in total disbelief. The shock began to flood my mind again and anguish flooded my heart and soul. It was real. God, why did I have to wake up? I didn't want to face this… not now… not ever. It's not fair. That son of a bitch!!!! I walked back upstairs to face Gary. He was in the shower. I grabbed his cell phone to listen to the messages again and found he had erased them along with many of the names I had previously seen on his contact list. Gary got out of the shower, dressed and left for work without even looking at me. We did not speak to each other for the next two days.

When Gary finally spoke to me he said, "The messages were from a lesbian woman with a deep voice."

"Not only are you going to lie to me, but you are going to insult my intelligence too? Since when have I been stupid?"

"I'm sorry. I shouldn't have ever given her my phone number."

"Let me talk to her or meet her."

He said he would try to set something up. A couple of days later, Gary told me that she didn't want to meet me and that if he persisted, she would sue him for sexual harassment on the job. I called him a lying faggot and told him that I knew it was a man.

"You like dick, plain and simple," I said.

Basically, for the next couple of weeks, I walked around in a fog. I couldn't sleep. I couldn't work. I cried all day long every day and wasn't able to be a mother to my son. Gary totally ignored me. He went to work everyday and came home later and later. I began to self-medicate with Benadryl, which allowed me to sleep for long hours. I couldn't stand the pain when I was awake and coherent. I wanted to be either unconscious or dead.

One day, when I couldn't take it anymore and realized that I felt suicidal and needed urgent help, I called my health insurance provider to make an appointment with a therapist. The intake receptionist could hear the desperation in my voice and set up an appointment for me within the next couple of hours. Sitting before the therapist I cried and cried as I told her my story. All she could say was "I am so sorry, I am so sorry." She diagnosed my condition as severe depression and made an appointment with the psychiatrist who prescribed anti-depressants and sleeping pills. Was this really me? I was the woman who always kept it together in every aspect of my life. How could I have become this broken, fearful, depressed, angry woman ready to end my life over a man—or is it a wo-man? This didn't happen to women like me. I was not a promiscuous woman sleeping with every guy that came around. Gary was not some stranger that I barely knew. I knew this man. I gave him my virginity years before. Little did I know he would take my innocence not once, but twice. I felt so violated and used. He said he loved me and I was his princess. I didn't picture my life as one more woman ending up single in the Fall of her life. I was supposed to enter my winter years with my lifelong companion, Gary.

During the next couple of months, as anger and rage brewed within me, I still tried to create a sense of normalcy for my son, not wanting him to ever know the pain and helplessness I felt. I kept going to work every day, but trying to concentrate was unbelievably torturous. My work performance suffered and I began to receive daily phone calls from my manager. In an attempt to salvage my job, I took an extended leave of absence, which exhausted all of my sick leave and vacation benefits. I started feeling anxious and frantic about how to keep my life moving forward while my mind was in a vice grip. I had to determine in my mind not to lose all that I had worked for and that included my 23 years of service in my government job.

While I worked frantically trying to live in an impossible situation, Gary continued his life as if nothing had ever happened. Every night while I lay next to Gary, I cried myself to sleep, and every morning, I woke to the reality of my shattered life. Most times, before Gary left for work, I stood before him begging for answers, needing an explanation, but he just ignored me. He would walk out of the door telling me to have a nice day as I stood there with my eyes filled with pain, wearing the same pajamas I had had on for three days. I would begin to walk around my house trying to get my mind to focus on something… anything. I would attempt to clean my beautiful dream house, but found myself sitting and crying instead. What was I going to do? I was supposed to be a wife and I had been a damn good one! I was supposed to fulfill all my dreams and goals with Gary. Now, I was alone and on my own again even though I still carried his name, cooked his food, and lived in the same house with him. It all seemed surreal, but visions would invade my mind of Gary doing vile things with men and I knew it was real.

During my darkest hour, I wrote the following and handed it to him when he came home from work:

Dear Gary,

I need to put my feelings into words before I crack up. I am dead inside. I feel like I no longer exist. My soul, my spirit, that essence that makes me Janine, is gone. I am still here physically, but my spirit is gone. I have no faith in God, humanity, the world. Everything I ever believed in, is no more.

I thought, just this once, that God was looking down upon me and blessed me with you. The timing was perfect; everything was just right. I loved you like an extension of myself. I was finally one; I was whole. I felt like I could conquer the world with you by my side. I had the love of my life back and I was finally happy and at peace. I could finally hear a love song and understand the words. They were singing about m—about us. Our love was pure, unconditional, beautiful, perfect—or so I thought.

But as always, life takes a cruel turn. Who was I to believe in love? Who was I to believe in happily ever after? I was stupid yet again. I got used. I got played. I will never trust myself again, but how could I, because I no longer exist? Only the shell of my physical body remains. When it is time for me to die, my body will stop; that's because my soul is already dead. No one can hurt me or use me again, because I no longer exist. They can't hurt what is no longer there. I am dead.

After reading this letter, Gary sat down on the side of our bed and sobbed with his head in his hands. Here I stood, perplexed again. Finally Gary had shown some type of emotion. I may never know what he felt, because he never uttered a word about that letter. He went back into hiding, like "down-low" men have taught themselves to do.

One part of me still loved him and the man I thought he was, but the betrayed part of me wanted to call his precious job and all of our so-called friends and tell them his secret. Obviously, he didn't give a damn about me, so why should I care about him? My mind raced, trying to validate my thoughts and why I should, and how I could get revenge in every way possible, but I kept hearing a voice from my upbringing say, "Vengeance belongs to the Lord."

Gary's decision to stay true to his deception caused an unbearable tension between us. One day, during a heated argument, Gary said, "Janine, I will never tell you the truth." With that, I realized the hopelessness of my marriage. My emotions were so raw that I felt as if I had been literally ripped to shreds. I couldn't think anymore. Soon, Gary began to see another woman and would purposely leave incriminating evidence of his affair in plain sight. I would accuse, he would deny. Pretty soon, just as he wanted, my focus left the men he was sleeping with and became fixated on this woman. I even called the woman and warned her that he was on the "down-low," just to find out that Gary had told her that I was crazy and taking psychiatric medication, so my warning fell on deaf ears. Gary began to take trips out of town for two and three days at a time. I later found out he was taking her along with him.

In an effort to release some of the agony I felt, I began to search the Internet looking for the answers my own husband wouldn't give me. To my dismay, I didn't find any answers. There were no websites or support groups dedicated to the plight of women in my situation. I felt so helpless and alone. One day, I was surfing a message board and came across a post written by a down-low brother. His post basically said he saw nothing wrong with the deception of his lifestyle and it was his business only, and not his fiancé's, if he slept with men. In a rage, I replied to his post, telling him how my life was turned upside down by my own husband's deception and how he should tell his pregnant fiancé the truth. He did not reply to my post. However, I did receive a compassionate e-mail from another woman who was living with the same reality. She gave me her telephone number and told me to call her at any time. The next morning, after Gary left for work, I dialed her number. We talked for hours and have been talking ever since. She has been my friend and is my co-author.

◇◇◇

Together we vowed that we would dedicate our lives to helping other women that would find themselves victims of down-low men. We were both committed to using this unthinkable experience to better the lives of others as we healed and gained our own self worth.

The same way the men also abandoned natural relations with women and were inflamed with lust for one another, men committed indecent acts with other men, and received in themselves the due penalty for their perversion. Furthermore, since they did not think it worthwhile to retain the knowledge of God, he gave them over to a depraved mind to do what ought not to be done.

—Romans 1:27, 28

"Love At First Sight"

Nadine & Gerome

It was August 1986 and I was starting my sophomore year in college. I was excited and ready to meet the new guys on campus. I remember being in the cafeteria with girls from my freshman year. We were eating and talking when I happened to glance up to see this fine brother who I just had to have. I asked the girls to look at him and check him out. They thought he was just "alright," but he was Adonis to me, so I looked a lot harder and deeper than they did.

I was uncomfortable approaching guys, so one of my girls said something to him. She introduced us and it was on from there. The only time he and I were not together was when we had class, other than that we were inseparable. I used to sneak him into my dorm room so we could have sex. I knew this was the man I wanted to spend the rest of my life with.

We were so happy and we had much fun together. We attended college for one more year and stopped. I went home to Atlanta for a couple of months and he found us an apartment in North Carolina, where we attended school. We had nothing materially, but who cared? We had each other.

We went on like the average young couple, trying to make it on minimum wage. Come hell or high water, we would go to the club and turn it out every weekend. Sometimes we would be checking our pockets for change to go to the club. We started the party. It was like the other clubheads were waiting for us to get out there and get things rockin'. Gerome would always have to pull me out on the dance floor because I was shy and he was the outgoing one. I sometimes got a little winded and had to sit down, but he would still be on the dance floor either dancing with someone else or by himself.

After a while, I got tired of going to the club every weekend, so sometimes he went alone. I didn't care until the weekend clubbing started turning into weekday clubbing. I was somewhat concerned, but I never asked questions, even though I had several floating around in my head.

At the time I was working at a convenience store/gas station. I was working with this guy who was quite effeminate. He was cool. I never gave his mannerisms a second thought. We got to be really good friends. One Saturday he asked me to hang out with him and I asked if my man could come and he was like, "the more the merrier." Well, we met up.

My man and my friend from work already knew each other, but I didn't know this. Those two played it off like two seasoned pros. Later, I found out that they didn't mess with each other, but they would hook each other up with other men. That night we went to a gay club. Were they trying to tell me something? I went inside and observed a lot of men dancing with each other. There were very few women and the women that were there looked extremely masculine. Obviously, I was really naïve for all I could think about was the jammin' music. We came out of that club at 6 a.m. I had a good time.

That was the first and last time I went out with the "guys." My man continued to go out without me at times. Eventually, he got what he really wanted and went out clubbin' without me. Did I have questions? Yes. Did I ask them? No. I carried on like nothing was different, but it was.

I was working at the store one Saturday preparing to end my shift. A classmate of my man came in the store. I spoke just to acknowledge her presence. You see, I didn't like or dislike this girl, but I knew she had a little girlie crush on my man. She came at me straight and said she had to something to tell me. I sort of got in defense mode and waited for whatever she was going to say. She wanted to talk somewhere a little more private, so she told me she would wait for me to get off work.

I walked outside and she was waiting in the parking lot. I was ready for anything this girl was going to say, but I wasn't ready for her to tell me that my man was gay!! I didn't act like I was surprised. I kept a poker face and said, "okay." I slid into the driver's seat of my car, started it, backed up and drove off.

I was cool until I arrived home. I went in, put my keys on the table and flopped down on the sofa. I grabbed the remote control and turned on the TV. CNN popped up. A camera panned slowly around, showing thousands of people. The next thing I knew another camera zoomed in on my man and another guy standing behind him.

That is when it hit me! I could see it as clear as day. He looked like a gay man with his lover adoringly standing behind him. I felt sick. That night, I waited anxiously for Gerome to come home. He was shocked when I greeted him with tears and profanity. I screamed at him, begging for the truth, for the next three hours. At first he denied, denied, denied. After a final barrage of questions and name-calling, Gerome finally came clean and told me the truth…that he was gay.

I called my mother and told her I had to come home. Of course, she wanted to know what was wrong, but I was too ashamed to tell her. My mother lived an hour away so the trip was no big deal; plus I needed to drive and get away from the place he and I called home, where we had conceived our child. Yes, I was pregnant, but I didn't know until a month later. Oh my God! What was I going to do now? Should I have an abortion? Should I carry this baby to term and then put him/her up for adoption? Should I keep my child and be the best mother I can be? Yes.

We lived together throughout my pregnancy, but we were not the usual happy couple with a child on the way. He tried to pretend everything was normal by being very attentive—all I had to do was ask and it was done, but this whole thing was abnormal and very painful for me. I was determined that my child was going to have both parents at home, regardless of what was going on.

We slept in separate rooms because *we* were over. I actually thought I could do this until he brought a man to our home. Can you believe it? It never occurred to me to bring another man home and disrespect him, but he had no problem doing it to me.

One early morning when I got up to go to the bathroom, I bumped into something in the dark hallway and got to swinging. This thing started hollering every time I landed a blow. This thing fought back, but I proceeded to beat it. During a brief intermission, I flipped on the light. There the thing was—standing in front of me in some silky-looking boxers.

"Who the hell are you?!" he asked me defensively.

"This is my damn house, so who the hell are you?" I yelled back. We started fighting again. Finally, my ex came out of his room dressed in his silky boxers too. I asked him what was going on. He didn't answer me immediately, but turned to the guy and asked him why he was fighting me. They verbally went back and forth for a minute and then the guy got dressed and left. I returned to my bed, but could not sleep as my mind was buzzing, thinking about what had just occurred.

Gerome got up early the next morning to go to Chicago. Later that morning, an eviction notice was placed on our door. He'd used the rent money for his trip! I went to the manager to try to save our home. Fortunately, the assistant manager was in. We were cool, so I told her what happened and she gave me the keys to a vacancy. All of the utilities were on so all I had to do was get my furniture. I rented the biggest truck I could get so I could make one trip. I took everything except his clothes. If I could have taken the lint off of the carpet I would have.

I was so done with my ex. Of course, by this time my son was born. I felt overwhelmed, but at the same time I felt like a failure because his father was no longer a part of us. I grew up without my dad for the better part of my life and I didn't like it. I didn't blame my mother one bit for my fatherless childhood, but I didn't want my child to grow up like I did. If my ex had disclosed to me that he had any inkling that he was gay, our relationship would not have lasted five long years, with a child right at the tail end of it.

After we parted ways, Gerome and I became friends. I must admit that I never felt so betrayed and disrespected in all of my life, but I also felt like it was my fault that my ex was gay. I was blaming myself for not being the woman he deserved. Essentially, I was beating myself up. But damn, he didn't want a woman anyway!!

I came to grips with it and moved on because whatever I felt was irrelevant. As long as we were excellent parents to our child, our personal lives did not matter. We had a son. As my son grew up, I was wondering how in the world I was going to tell him that his father is a gay man. I would stand over my son while he was in his crib and cry. I would apologize to him over and over again. He would lie there in the crib kicking and laughing. I did not want to be a single mother with a child. I was raised like this and it was diffi-cult for my mother. I actually got scared, but knew I had to get my priorities straight.

As my son started to get older that question came into mind again: how would I tell my son that his father is gay? I didn't want him to find it out from someone else. Well, my son is a teenager now and he knows about his father being gay. His father told him a couple of years ago, at my request. I did not want my son to find out in the street, like I did. According to my son, his father cried when trying to tell him. Was this a feeling of guilt? Was he ashamed of what he was? Or was he looking for some kind of empathy from his son?

Later on, my son asked me the hardest question I thought that I would ever hear, "Momma, do you think I am gay?" My heart fell into the pit of my stomach. I didn't know how to answer that. Being a firm believer that being gay is a choice; this is what I told him, that it is his choice. We talked briefly about homosexuality in general. When I concluded our talk and told him that I loved him unconditionally no matter what, we embraced and went on like normal.

Since my ex and I split, I had been in a few rocky relationships and I had a daughter in between. So just like my own mother, I am raising two children as a single mother. I am in a six- soon to be seven-year relationship with a man that I know I truly love. He is my rock. I must admit I wish I'd met this man 13 years ago. My life would have definitely been different.

So why all the secrecy, lies, deceit, and ultimately, disrespect from the down-lows? Are they ashamed of what they are doing? Some aren't because they don't think they are wrong. Well, it is wrong and we women need to stop making excuses in our heads for "abnormal" things that we see and feel.

◇◇◇

We need to speak up and ask questions when in doubt. Until we do, we will always be subjected to STDs and the worst of them all: HIV/AIDS. We have got to wake up and protect ourselves now, because later could be fatal.

I consider myself a survivor. I have dealt with a lot of pain and heartache, but I have overcome my obstacles. My hope is to help other women by telling my story and ultimately we can affect the stop of the spread of HIV/AIDS and other STDs. Women, please be honest with yourselves and stop making excuses when you know something is wrong. Listen to your gut—it never lies to you.

Finally, please protect yourself. If you don't, do not depend on someone else to do it for you. Having unprotected sex is like signing a death warrant.

Peace and much love to my sisters.

Do you not know that the wicked will not inherit the kingdom of God? Do not be deceived: Neither the sexually immoral nor idolaters nor adulterers nor male prostitutes nor homosexual offenders nor thieves nor the greedy nor drunkards nor slanderers nor swindlers will inherit the kingdom of God.

—I Corinthians 6:9–10

"Southern Comfort"

Saundra & James

I was a 16-year-old girl having issues with my mother. Our relationship left me yearning for love—from anyone. Of course my mother loved me, but she was dealing with issues of her own, which I didn't understand at the time—who does at 16? To replace the lack of time she spent with me, Mom would overindulge me with material things, like fashionable clothes and a car.

At 16 I felt awkward and ugly. All my girlfriends had gotten their period and some had even had sex. I'd had neither and felt left out. My best friend was a "red bone" (name for light-skinned Black people); she was a cheerleader with a nice body and beautiful face. I could not believe that this was my best friend. Later, I realized that the reason she was my best friend was so that she could borrow my clothes, ride in my car, and say insulting things to me, knowing I would still hang around. I needed the attention my friend gave me, so I didn't mind the fact that she used me.

I started working at the local southern restaurant named "Hardee's." One day, I was taking an order and *he* walked in. He was short, bowlegged, and handsome with Indian hair. His skin was smooth and a shade down from "red bone." I could not believe this fine guy was standing at my cash register. I also noticed a sexy gap between his two front teeth. I fell in love in that instant. We became friends, which in my mind meant he was my boyfriend. Once I came back to reality, I realized it was a one-sided relationship, so I went my way and he went his. I continued to work at the restaurant and he continued to come in, but he wouldn't come to my register.

Time moved on and I graduated from high school. I was growing up and finally liked the woman I was becoming. I didn't go on to college because the importance of education was never discussed in our home. My world consisted of working and clubbing. One day, while working at a textile plant, my mother approached me and told me she had found an apartment in town, but it was only big enough for one. She then suggested that I go into the military. She had suggested this many times before, but I would just brush it off. Feeling unloved by anyone, even my own mother, I decided to enlist in the army and with tears flowing down my face, I gave an oath to become their property for the next three years.

While in the army, I got pregnant and married my first husband. We had a beautiful son. Three months into our marriage, the army shipped him overseas, leaving me alone once again. After being apart from my husband for a year and a half, I was finally shipped overseas to join him. However, I was not the same little girl he had married, and neither was he the same boy. We tried a few more months and later separated. After fulfilling my obligation to the military, I was discharged. Feeling low and defeated, I returned to my hometown and went right back to my same old clubbing ways.

One Sunday night at my favorite club, I was dancing when I noticed a figure at the bar. It was him—James—my first love from Hardee's. I had a couple of drinks to boost my confidence and then I approached him. I asked him if he remembered me and he said he did. I asked him to dance, so we did and spent the rest of the night together at the club. At closing time, I offered him a ride home. Once at his house, we sat outside and talked a while. I told him I had a son and he said he had daughter who he had not seen in three years. We exchanged phone numbers and I steadied myself for that long-awaited kiss, just to receive a quick peck on the cheek. I thought to myself, ooohhh, a man with chivalry!

He moved into my apartment and from that night on, we played house for three years. I would come home from work to a spotless house with hot food on the stove. He never gave me money and I never asked for it. I was just satisfied with him keeping our house clean and being good to my son. When it came to lovemaking, there was no passion and he didn't really seem to want to cuddle or be affectionate. I always felt like he was giving me only a part of himself while I was giving him all of me. About a year into our relationship, we were watching football together one afternoon when I noticed him just staring at me. When I looked into his eyes, he said, "You are going to give me a son." I felt flattered, but just blew it off because I thought I was incapable of having any more children due to a prior illness. It turned out I was wrong because about a year later, I gave him that son.

The whole time I was pregnant, James seemed aloof. He hardly stayed with me at night anymore, choosing instead to stay at the home of an older man who he described as being like a father to him. I would see him on a daily basis, but things had changed. Something else—or should I say some*one* else—had caught his attention. Toward the end of my pregnancy, I heard rumors that my man was caught with another man at his job. I asked him what that was about and he just laughed and said someone was playing a joke on him. I cannot remember exactly what he said, but for the moment, his explanation comforted me, even though I felt I was losing him. He was so indifferent toward me that he was not even present when I gave birth to our son. Sure, he showed up a couple of days later, but I knew then that I had already lost him. Before long, James stopped coming home at all.

After what seemed like forever, he started coming around now and then to check up on his son. He always came empty-handed. All of a sudden his attention turned toward me again and he started staying overnight. We seemed to go back to our old routine, only now there were two kids to deal with instead of one. In the meantime, he had gone back to the church and now considered himself "saved," and me a tramp or something similar, because I had been married once before. I would let these hurtful words slide, even though every mean word pierced my heart. He then started to spend a lot of time with the pastor's son. I didn't think much of that and thought maybe this guy would be a good influence on James, because he also was married with two kids. Then I started hearing things like this guy used to dress like a "faggot" and like a woman. I also heard rumors that the old man James used to visit was gay. However, whenever I asked questions about these rumors, he would laugh and tell me they were lies. I believed him, of course.

One day James announced that he wanted to see his little girl. I had seen pictures of Chelsea, but had never met her. James had not seen her in years and now felt an urgency to find her, for some reason. Not knowing where she lived, we started on a journey that took us from one city to the next. We loaded up the car and were ready to drive off when I realized I had forgotten my makeup case and ran back inside to get it. When I returned to the car, James was reading a letter and began to quickly fold it up when I walked up on him. I asked him what he was reading and like always, he just brushed me off. We rode in silence as I thought about that letter. When we reached our first destination, Chelsea's grandmother's house, James got out of the car and walked up to the door. Right away I went for his wallet that was left on the seat and started reading that letter. I was hurt as I read it because this woman was saying how much she loved my man and that she accepted his being with me. The letter also said, "I bought you those shoes you wanted." Little did I know that my hurt would turn to devastation because as I got to the closing, I saw the words, "*Love Mike.*" I sat there in shock, staring at the name, so in a zone that I didn't hear James when he approached the car. He looked at me and then took the paper from my hand, folded it up and put it back in his wallet. We drove away in silence again, never mentioning the letter—not even once. We eventually found his daughter, spent a few days with her, and went back home.

When we got back into town he told me to drop him off at the pastor's son's house and I did just that. I rode home still in a state of disbelief. I cried all night long, ravaged with pain. The next morning I called my mother at her job and blurted out to her, "I gotta get an AIDS test, I've been sleeping with a "faggot." I then told her about the letter. She didn't say anything because she never liked James from the start.

That letter signified the end of the relationship for me. James was no longer my man. In fact, I didn't see him as a man at all. I was so numb and felt like such a fool that I felt more defeated than ever before. I couldn't seem to think and could barely take care of my children. My concentration was so bad that one day I rear-ended a car…. I thought my car was in reverse when it was really in drive. At times I looked at my son and wondered how I would tell him that his father was gay and would rather live with a man than with us. For a long time I never revealed his dirty secret to anyone else. I suffered in silence. However, after hearing negative things he was spreading about me, I told anyone who would listen that he slept with men. The more I talked about it the more relieved I felt.

◇◇◇

It has been 18 years since I found out James was on the down-low. I have moved on with my life, but James' deception caused me to have trust issues with everyone, especially men. The experience made me feel used and dirty. I have had three AIDS tests and so far I am clean. Although James and I have had contact over the years because of our son, he has still never admitted that he is gay, or said he was sorry for hurting me. He even accused me of wanting him back. I laughed in his face. Unfortunately, he is now married to another unsuspecting victim and they have a child together. I felt sorry for the woman because she married a stranger who creeps around with other men. Sure enough, a few years into their marriage I received an e-mail from her asking me questions about James' strange behavior. I told her the truth; however, she is still in denial, just as I once was.

It is actually reported that there is sexual immorality among you, and of a kind that does not occur even among pagans: A man has his father's wife. And you are proud! Shouldn't you rather have been filled with grief and have put out of your fellowship the man who did this? Even though I am not physically present, I am with you in spirit. And I have already passed judgment on the one who did this, just as if I were present. When you are assembled in the name of our Lord Jesus and I am with you in spirit, and the power of o5ur Lord Jesus is present, hand this man over to Satan, so that the sinful nature may be destroyed and his spirit saved on the day of the Lord. Your boasting is not good. Don't you know that a little yeast works through the whole batch of dough? Get rid of the old yeast that you may be a new batch without yeast—as you really are. For Christ, our Passover lamb, has been sacrificed. Therefore let us keep the Festival, not with the old yeast, the yeast of malice and wickedness, but with bread without yeast, the bread of sincerity and truth.

—1 Corinthians 5:1–8

"God Is Faithful"

Sabrina & Steve

I believe that back in the day, many of our young men were raised to find a good woman, and part of the good woman package was that she had a good job or the ability to obtain one. I truly believe that part of my husband's attraction to me was the fact that I was independent, a hard worker, loyal—in short, I was good for PR and his American dream image, complete with white picket fence. My story is not simple, as my husband, Steve, told me that he had practiced the homosexual lifestyle in the past. However, he assured me that God had delivered him and he was more than capable of having a loving relationship with a woman.

As I look back, there were telltale signs, but in my ignorance I didn't recognize them. I didn't actually catch him—it was more intuition than anything. My dilemma caused me to pray to God to help me find the truth or else I would go mad. Why didn't I recognize the telltale signs? Because he always had a reason that fit my belief system enough to throw me off his scent, at least, until the next slip-up or questionable glance, lingering hug or overly friendly interest in certain males. Also, there was always an effeminate male in the background.

The straw that broke the camel's back was when I told a female friend my suspicions and concerns. She sensed my struggle and how it was affecting me, especially since there was no factual evidence that was sufficient to satisfy my suspicions. She arranged a meeting between me and a man who was a former employee of my husband's company. He asked me how much did I want to know and I replied, "Everything." He asked me if I was sure. I braced myself and nodded 'yes'. He took me line upon line, precept upon precept, about how my husband tried to get him to participate in homosexual play. He told me that Steve showed him pornographic material behind closed doors under the pretense of having a staff meeting. He said that my husband even begged him to simply show him his penis. He wouldn't rub it, suck it, or anything, Steve just wanted to see it. Now, how mad is that??!! This gentleman struggled to tell me the truth as he saw the blood leave my face. He told me that he had to leave the company and even changed his phone number to stop my husband from harassing him for sex. He said that he was strong enough to resist Steve's advances, but Craig, another employee, didn't seem quite as strong. You see, my husband played on the insecurities of other men. These men would confide a damning secret to Steve, and he would turn around and use that very secret to manipulate them. That manipulation soon turned to seduction. I had already determined that our marriage was over, but what happened next felt like an answer from God.

A few weeks after being told of my husband's secret homosexual escapades on the job, I was called into my pastor's study where he sadly informed me that there had been multiple reports of my husband trying to pick up men in the congregation. I was told that Steve had made subtle comments that were sexual in nature that left the men feeling funny. The pastor told me there were five men who had reported to him about Steve trying to seduce them. This was very humiliating because my husband was also a minister at the church. Guys had confessed their struggle with feelings of homosexuality with Steve and he betrayed their confidence, abused his position, and used their secrets to set up his own homosexual network in the congregation. I was appalled, humiliated, and sick to my stomach. It's one thing to do this cruel thing to me, but to disrespect God enough to use his ministerial standing and his authority in the church to fuel his own perversion was reprehensible. Needless to say, after all of this I had to get away. I left the church and had no desire to go to any church in that city. I was so paranoid, feeling like I was wearing a scarlet letter that said *"fool"* and that everyone was whispering behind my back.

◇◇◇

I am still healing, but God is faithful and I know that I will heal and be all right. As long as I remain anonymous, you ladies may use my story in your book in order that it might help another woman.

"Everything is permissible for me"—but not everything is beneficial. "Everything is permissible for me"—but I will not be mastered by anything. "Food for the stomach and the stomach for food"—but God will destroy them both. The body is not meant for sexual immorality, but for the Lord, and the Lord for the body. By his power God raised the Lord from the dead, and he will raise us also. Do you not know that your bodies are members of Christ himself? Shall I then take the members of Christ and unite them with a prostitute? Never! Do you not know that he who unites himself with a prostitute is one with her in body? For it is said, "The two will become one flesh." But he who unites himself with the Lord is one with him in spirit. Flee from sexual immorality. All other sins a man commits are outside his body, but he who sins sexually sins against his own body. Do you not know that your body is a temple of the Holy Spirit, who is in you, whom you have received from God? You are not your own; you were bought at a price. Therefore honor God with your body.

—I Corinthians 6:12–20

"Desperately In Denial"

Keisha & Anthony

I met Anthony at a church singles retreat in May 1998. I was looking for a seat and just as I began to sit down, the chair was suddenly occupied by this tall, handsome, cocoa brown, brother. For a moment, I thought I was playing musical chairs, with the handsome stranger winning the game. Through the rest of the weekend activities I noticed him watching me from a distance and our eyes met a few times; however, he never made any attempt to approach me. The retreat was a big success, giving me just what I needed and I returned home renewed, empowered, and encouraged.

The very next Sunday at church, there he was again. We began to flirt with each other at church functions and this continued throughout the summer, but he never asked me out. One Sunday in July, I finally got up the courage and invited him to dinner and he declined, stating he had issues. The next Sunday he asked me if I was cooking dinner and I said yes. He then invited himself over saying we could watch the football game together. I rushed home and prepared a quick meal and when he came over that night, we chatted during dinner, then moved into the living room to watch the game. The next thing I knew, Anthony was snoring. He slept all night on the couch and I slept on the loveseat across the room.

We talked on the phone every night from July until December, but we never went on a formal date. The death of my sister happened to coincide with the death of a close relative of Anthony's and the grief we shared seemed to bond us together in a special way. One day, during a phone conversation, Anthony told me he loved me and it came at a time when I needed it the most. When I returned home from my sister's funeral, I forced myself to get back into my normal routine, which included my blossoming relationship with Anthony. Our courtship consisted of telephone conversations and him coming over to my house, but we *still* never went on any formal dates. The only time I was ever invited to Anthony's apartment was when I took him to pick up some of his belongings.

It was in February when our conversation turned toward marriage. Here was a 30-year-old man with a military career, no children, who had never married, and who actually attended my church. He loved children, which was wonderful because I was the single mom of a five-year-old daughter. I could see a future with this man. The next month I went to North Carolina to visit my family and Anthony went with me. While there, to my surprise, Anthony got on his knee and proposed to me with a ring and everything.

Later, I found out he had gone to my father first and asked for my hand; so when he proposed my entire family was there. My family loved him because he was so respectful. He even stayed with friends instead of in my family's home and we all took that as a sign of his respect for me. We had a military wedding and as I walked down the aisle and the soldiers lifted their sabers, I noticed everyone crying, including Anthony. Our vows were very spiritual. My wedding was like a fairy tale with the swords, horse and carriage, everything. I felt like Cinderella. The reception was just as wonderful and afterward we spent our first night together. As we talked and opened our gifts and cards, I thought about how blessed I was. All that was left was to consummate our marriage; but again, Anthony went to sleep.

We made love the next morning, but it was nothing to write home about. I was very disappointed and I was also surprised, because he had told me what a freak he was in bed; but his lovemaking was so mechanical. There was no passion, which left me feeling very empty and confused.

The next morning we went to Virginia Beach for our honeymoon. That night, he made love to me again and this time it felt real. It was true, it was intimate. Our honeymoon lasted for four more days and during this time I realized my husband was not very romantic. We spent the remainder of our honeymoon test-driving SUVs, talking, and eating out.

The marriage started to fall apart as soon as we got home. It began with his criticism of my housekeeping. I would make the bed and he would remake it. He would get upset if the vacuum cleaner lines were not going in the same direction. He claimed my closet was messy and not color-coordinated. He would complain if I left my curling iron out. My daughter could not even dance in the living room because it would mess up the vacuum cleaner lines. We argued constantly about the house. After a month of marriage, I found out I was pregnant, which made Anthony very happy because he had no kids of his own. This is when our sex life stopped completely. Whenever I tried to initiate lovemaking, he always said he was tired. I became not only disenchanted, but also suspicious. I couldn't understand why, after only a month of marriage, the same man that cried at the altar, was now so emotionally distant and cold. I thought those tears had been from happiness, but now I wasn't so sure.

One night, about four months later, I woke up from my sleep and something said to me, "Go check his cell phone voicemail." I listened to the voicemail and there was a man's voice telling my husband that he admired his penis. I fell apart. I cried for hours and then I called my cousin and cried some more. I woke Anthony up and let him hear the message. He looked like a scared child. He promised me nothing had happened and nothing ever would happen. I told him that if he meant what he said, then we needed to get another phone number. The next day we changed his cell phone number.

For the next year, everything seemed okay. Every time I thought about the incident, I pushed it to the back of my mind. As a matter of fact, for the next two years, we never talked about it and I never mentioned it. It wasn't until our third year of marriage that I had to confront the issue again.

Things seemed to have gone from bad to worse. I began to notice a big change in my husband. In fact, he wanted nothing to do with me. There were nights I *begged* him for sex, but he showed me no mercy. One night after taking a shower, I asked him to make love to me, but he said he would no longer make love to me because he found my body repulsive. This comment wounded me deeply and I cried myself to sleep. After all, I worked out three times a week at the gym and was always careful with my diet. I knew my body was in great shape. Other men would always comment on how fine I was, so how could my own husband find my body so repulsive?

Anthony's new job had him going to work at 4:30 a.m. and one morning on the way to work, he got into an accident and totaled the truck. I had to go to the salvage yard to retrieve our personal items from the truck and while I was cleaning it, I found a hotel receipt with a man's name on it. I rushed home and got on the computer, and went to "Anywho.com," and found out the man's phone number and address. I then called the Internet company and because I was the master account holder, I was able to obtain Anthony's password. I went to his buddy-list and saw the long list of male names. I pretended to be Anthony and went to the chat room that was listed on his favorite places.

Many of the men in the chat room came right out and asked me for sex. That's when I realized that all of his buddies were gay or men on the down-low. The next thing I read was an e-mail from the very guy on the hotel receipt. He didn't really give much away in his e-mail, but his closing statement read *"Think Good Thoughts."* About an hour later, Anthony called to check on me and when I told him goodbye, I said *"Think Good Thoughts."* The next thing I knew, Anthony was back at home because he realized I knew. When I showed him the list of men, he lied again saying they were all old army buddies and that one of their names must have been linked to the gay site. I accepted his lie because I didn't want to destroy my perfect family. Later that night, my husband really went out of his way to make love to me, but guilt was written all over his face. Again, I willed myself to accept what had happened because it was so hard for me to believe that a man who had married me, conceived a child with me and called himself my husband, could really be gay.

A few months later, we bought a new house and our life appeared to be back on track. Anthony tried to make me believe that he worked many hours at his new job, but in reality he had a lot of free time on his hands. All of a sudden, I began to see a lot of strange numbers on our cell phone bill again. I called the numbers and they were all men. When I questioned Anthony about the numbers, he blew me off and started using his work cell phone instead of his personal cell phone, but soon his job put a stop to that and he started using his own cell phone once more. I also went into the computer hard drive and retrieved all of his downloads, only to find pictures of erect penises from men that sent him e-mails. I felt like such a fool. How could I have believed he would change? The only thing he changed was his attitude toward me. I started eating more and gaining weight from the emotional stress.

Eventually, the real Anthony emerged and he started to meet the on-line men in person. He even started having a relationship with one of them, named Charles. Throughout it all, we were still attending church faithfully and portraying the happy family. Although I was still in church, I started drinking every night in an attempt to self-medicate. Anthony became so caught up in his secret lifestyle that when Christmas rolled around, I could hear him upstairs calling these guys to wish them a merry Christmas, oblivious that I was downstairs listening. Right after Christmas, I went to

North Carolina to visit my family and the first night I left, my husband spent the night away from home. I found out because he forgot the code to the burglar alarm and had to call me to get it. I asked him how he got into the house the night before and he got angry, defensive and hung up the phone in my ear. I returned home that day, but Anthony did not come home for that entire weekend. When he returned, he stayed home a few nights, but then, without explanation, he packed a bag, left, and moved in with Charles for the longest, most humiliating, and painful nine months of my life. While I was at work every day, my husband was creeping back home, moving his things out little by little, as if I wouldn't notice.

Through it all, I tried to keep my dignity. I never went to his job, caused any public scenes or anything that would be embarrassing to him. I suffered in silence. No one knew, except my best friend. Soon, depression grabbed me with a death grip and I went into a numb state. I cried all day and night and even checked out on my children. So many times, I thought of taking my own life. Trying to keep from going insane, I slept with my Walkman on at night with sermons playing in my ears. I have surrendered totally to God now. I had backslidden, but God gathered me into his loving arms.

During the nine months that Anthony was away, he had separation papers drawn up. He kept saying we had marital issues and that he could no longer live with me. Then suddenly, he came home, saying he loved me and that he had changed. I believed God had answered my prayers. In an effort to rekindle our marriage, we took a trip to the Poconos and I thought everything was fine. Two months later, he started interacting with Charles again. I knew because I had checked his e-mail and Charles's number was on his cell phone bill. I also found a Valentine's Day card from Charles telling Anthony how much he loved him. I read text messages from Anthony to Charles and he actually called this man, "Baby." One day, Charles sent Anthony an e-mail stating that their love was God-given love and begged my husband not to end what they had. I confronted

Anthony about it and of course he lied again. He said he didn't know Charles was in love with him and that if he was, he surely didn't believe it was true.

◇◇◇

A few weeks later, I found a letter, which revealed that my husband had been treated for Chlamydia. I went to my doctor and sure enough, I tested positive for Chlamydia. I finally broke down that day. I sobbed for two hours and told the doctor everything. After I got home from the doctor's, I confronted Anthony with the letter and he actually had the nerve to deny it. After about an hour of my crying and yelling, he finally admitted he was having sex with men. Finally... a confession... but I am still here.

And no wonder, for Satan himself masquerades as an angel of light. It is not surprising, then, if his servants masquerade as servants of righteousness. Their end will be what their actions deserve.

—I Corinthians 11:14–15

"Shattered"

Summer & Kenneth

I am a 43-year-old woman who was born and raised in Philadelphia, PA. I grew up with six brothers and sisters, who were all raised by my mother. My father left the family when I was 12 years old. It was hard on my mother who tried to do all she could for us. I was not a child who could be friendly with everyone. I used to listen to my mom and dad argue, day after day, about everything from money to other women. I learned at an early age to turn inside myself and not let anyone in. My mother used to say, "Summer is my strange child."

I only opened up when I was around my track team as these were the only people I felt comfortable with. I was into a lot of sports and tried to stay away from home as much as possible because home brought me a lot of pain. I couldn't understand why my mother was always angry. What had made her so bitter? She never had a kind word for those around her. Little did I know that she was slowly dying from a broken heart. It would be many years later that I would understand her pain.

I joined the army in 1983, and after my initial training I went to Germany. I became friends with a man who I will call Kenneth. We became very good friends, and later, lovers. I could tell by some of our talks that he had been through some type of pain in his young life even though we were only 21 years old. We did everything together. He was my confidant and I was his. As time went on I became pregnant. I went back to the states and he stayed in Germany. We planned to get married when his time was up in Germany. I went on with my life in a small town in Alabama. This is where my next tour of duty was. As my pregnancy progressed, Kenneth continued to write and call me. I was so happy—or so I thought. When Kenneth came to visit me in August of 1986, I was due to deliver any day. We made love as soon as we could even though I was big and very near delivery. I was as big as a house, but Kenneth still knew how to make me feel special.

Kenneth was right by my side when our son made his appearance into the world. When it was time to bring our son home from the hospital, his daddy was nowhere to been found. My best friend brought my son and me home from the hospital in a military vehicle. Kenneth called me later that day and told me he had to go home to his mother's house, but he would be back. I felt a little uncomfortable with that, but I shrugged it off. A couple of days later, he came back with his entire family. They really enjoyed the new baby. They stayed for a week. Kenneth had to go back to Germany and I went home with his mother. I stayed there with my son and I felt loved by his family. Little did I know that this was just a façade.

When I went back to Alabama four weeks later, I had to leave my son with Kenneth's mother. I was being sent to Korea and I knew my son could not go with me. One day while at work, I got a call back from my doctor who said he needed to see me. I did not worry as I thought it was something simple. Imagine my surprise when my doctor told me I had an STD. I was so hurt and shocked. I couldn't believe it. I knew I had only made love to Kenneth, so he had cheated on me and exposed me to a venereal disease. I called him in Germany and let him have it, but all he did was lie, lie, lie, and try to deny it. I told him I never wanted to see him again. Later that night, he called me back and said he was sorry.

I was not ready to forgive Kenneth so I went on with my life while my son still had to live with his grandmother. I went to Korea and had no contact with Kenneth. I still loved this man, but I was still so hurt. I spent a year in Korea and when I returned, I was sent to

Kentucky. I set up housing and later went to get my son. It was some time later that I found out that Kenneth had a woman pregnant at the same time I was pregnant. By this time I thought I was over him, but the awful truth of his betrayal smacked me in the face again. I swallowed my pride and tried to act like I didn't care, and again, life went on. Thank God I didn't marry him!!

A couple of years later I did get married and had a baby girl with my husband. There was still emptiness inside me because I felt like there was no closure. Even though I was married, I still wanted answers from Kenneth as to why he'd hurt me. There was a place inside me that my husband could not touch or heal. Eventually we grew apart and he found comfort in someone else's arms. I should have seen it coming, but I was totally blind-sided by our divorce. I had no idea that my second husband was cheating too. After the divorce, my son, who was now 15 years old, began to act out in school. I contacted his father by e-mail hoping to get him involved. All he had to say was, "What does your husband say about it?" I told him my husband and I were going through a divorce. He asked for my number and I gave it to him and sure enough, he called the next day. We talked for a long time. He told me he was sorry for hurting me all those years ago. We chalked it up to just being young. Anyway, Kenneth continued to call me everyday. He even kept in touch with our son. One night while we were talking, he told me he still loved me and I told him the same. I was still hurting from the divorce and I guess Kenneth knew this. *Easy prey.*

Kenneth was in the Middle East now and would not return until late summer and when he did he came straight to me. We fell in love all over again and I felt whole for the first time in years. He became a good father figure for my daughter, but for some reason my son kept his distance. He didn't trust his father and he didn't want me to become involved with him again. I guess he knew something I didn't. *Out of the mouths of babes.*

As the relationship progressed I felt so happy. I just knew this was right. We did everything together. Kenneth drove to see me every weekend. Six months into the relationship he asked me to marry him and I said 'yes'. He even put the ring on my finger on bent knee, just like it was supposed to be. When he told me that his mother and I needed to talk about the upcoming wedding, I didn't think it was strange because I knew how close he was to his mom. Everything was going great. We made a lot of plans together.

Kenneth was shipped back to Afghanistan and we continued to communicate by e-mail and phone. He had given me access to all his accounts and we bought furniture for the new life we would live together. When he returned from Afghanistan he went to his mother's house instead of mine. I had to drive there to see him. When I arrived, he seemed cold and distant. I was totally confused and scared as hell. I later discovered from an e-mail that was sent to me that Kenneth had fallen for a woman while there in Afghanistan. I confronted him and of course he lied. I had spoken to the woman and Kenneth still denied everything. When he did acknowledge that he had cheated, he never gave me a reason or any details as to why. Things were strained between us now; but again, I forgave him. We kept our wedding plans intact, but I never fully trusted him again.

My instincts were rattling my brain constantly and I was overwhelmed with suspicion. I started looking for answers myself and in the process, gained access to his cell phone. I would check his messages and hear all kinds of women leaving him messages. Kenneth was still cheating and still lying about it. Why was I surprised? Why did I feel confused and trapped? I had given him not a second, but a third chance with me and he was again hurting me.

As time went on Kenneth began to blatantly disrespect me. He would get angry for silly reasons. He would curse me and call me stupid. I did not know where all this was coming from. He would later tell me how sorry he was. I forgave him over and over again. I checked his cell phone constantly. I tried everything I could to be there for him. I thought I could change him.

Kenneth was then sent to Texas for nine months. He would fly me out to see him every month. We began to try to pull the relationship together. One day he called me and asked me to book him a flight to Dallas, Texas. He said he wanted to go see a basketball game with one of his male friends. I booked the flight, but I didn't believe him. I checked and found out that the game he talked about was actually being played in Memphis, Tennessee. So why was he in Dallas? Kenneth had gone to see another woman and he had me book the flight. Why would he hurt me so much? I could not reach him by his cell as he had turned it off. He would call when he could get away, but then I wouldn't answer. My heart was so broken. When I did talk to him, he accused me of not trusting him and he told me he was tired of trying to prove he loved me. He tried to blame me. He tried to tell me it was all in my head.

The next time I flew out to see Kenneth again, I noticed he was close to a male friend of his and had a picture of this guy and himself on his screen saver. They weren't doing anything out of the ordinary on the picture, but it made me feel uneasy for some reason. I asked him why this picture was on his screen saver and he said that his friend Troy had put it there. I said nothing else about it.

After spending nine months in Texas he was sent to a base in Georgia, which was about two hours from me; but he didn't come to see me that often. This was strange to me because we were close to each other in distance so why wouldn't he want to spend his time with me? One day he came to visit and I noticed blood on the back of his boxer shorts. I asked him about this and he said he was having trouble with hemorrhoids. On another occasion there was a lot of blood on my toilet seat. I thought my daughter was on her cycle, but when I asked her she said 'no'. I then asked Kenneth, and he said it was him...hemorrhoid trouble again.

I told him he needed to go to the hospital and that I would take him. He refused, so I called his mother and told her he was bleeding. She said to give him the phone. They talked, but it was strange. I felt a deep uneasiness in the pit of my stomach like something was not quite right. That is when I started to think back on a lot of things he had said and a lot of things he did. For instance, Kenneth would always bash gays and would openly criticize gay people. He seemed obsessed with gay comments. He later told me that he wanted to read a book his mother had. Lo and behold it was the book J.L. King had written about men on the down-low. I was confused. Why would a man want to read this book if he was not into this lifestyle? I *had* read the book and now I knew what he was trying to tell me, but he would not come out and say it. He once asked me had I ever thought about being with another woman. I was appalled. I told him 'of course not'. I am Catholic and we don't believe in this same sex madness. Kenneth was hoping I would say 'yes' so he could tell me about himself, but I didn't know it at the time. Just like a cheating narcissist, he tried to make me share in his guilt. When I started to send him literature about men on the down-low to see what he had to say, he never responded. He would talk about everything else I would send him, but never that.

In September 2006, I ended the relationship. It was too stressful. I was coming home from work one day and I just started to cry. I was driving and crying. A cop pulled me over and asked me had I been drinking. I replied no. He took a look at my face and asked me what was wrong. I cried and it all came flooding out. The police officer hugged me and told me I was in no shape to drive. He called his partner and they drove me home and brought my car home. He is a very good friend of mine, even today. He checked on me day-to-day, after this incident. I think it all came to light that my man was on the down-low. He would never be honest and tell me, but, I knew. How does a woman come back from this? I put up with being cheated on and lied to, disrespected by him and his mother. I think she also knew, but nobody told me. I felt raped. Kenneth took my right to choose my own destiny away from me. I had not been given the option to stay or go. I was shattered. I would cry every day. I would text him angry one minute and full of love the next. I was so very confused. I did not know what to do. Even when I told him I could not be with him anymore, his selfish narcissistic ways wouldn't let him believe it. Why should he? I had taken so much dirt and stayed this long. Why would I leave him now? I had finally come face to face with the truth: I had a cheating down-low man that also slept with women. This was the ultimate betrayal, and then his mother poured salt in the wound and said it was my fault because I let him cheat. Imagine that. She blamed me! Ladies, don't turn on each other over any man. Stand as the sisters you say you are. I needed a sister. Where were my sisters? Some of them were laughing at me and the rest just shook their heads and stayed as far away from me as they could.

I was so hurt. I had once again allowed this man to come into my life and hurt me. I wanted revenge, but it is not mine to take. He had not been honest and he led me to believe one thing when he not only felt another, but *was* another. I was devastated. This man is a soldier in the army and leads our troops. What kind of man can do this? I'll tell you what kind of man, the same kind of men that lived in Sodom and Gomorrah. When God sent his angels to Lot's house, these same men were so overwhelmed with homosexual lust that they came knocking on the door trying to get the male angels to come out so they could have sex, and the angels had to blind them to confuse them and render them helpless. *Sodom... that word never held much meaning for me until...*

Only now, when I look back, I see all the signs I didn't see before...the gay bashing, the tight pants he would sometimes wear, his fascination with new flashy clothing all the time, the different women he used as beards to cover his real desires. I will never allow myself to be used again. Of course, I have nothing at all to do with Kenneth, but still what I went through flashes through my mind every day and the wound still feels so raw. I did not want to die of AIDS because of a man. I am not willing to pay with my life. I struggle with this hurt and pain everyday. I surfed the net trying to find answers. I have to somehow come to grips with the pain this man caused me and my children. How could a man, I had given so much love to, hurt me so much.

◇◇◇

All this time I was blaming myself and thinking that I had somehow pushed him away; made him run from me. I look back now and see that he was running from himself. This man is using women to cover his secret as you would an unmade bed by throwing the quilt over the dirty sheets to make everything look clean on top. Now I just feel empty inside and completely shattered.

Part Two
The Warning Signs

What are the Signs?

Down-low men purposely avoid looking or acting feminine. They try to portray themselves as strong and masculine in a deliberate effort to exterminate any doubt of their heterosexuality. Therefore, in today's world, a woman cannot determine a man's sexuality by his mannerisms or style of dress alone. The motive of the down-low man's heart is to have the sexual gratification that he seeks from other men, while still protecting his macho image on the surface. If you recall, some of the personal ads in the profiles we listed earlier, specifically requested "masculine men, only." Some specifically stated, "no femmes." So, ladies, you can't get a good read on any man's sexual lifestyle, character, integrity, or heart by the way he looks. Just because he looks and acts masculine does not mean he is not on the down-low.

"What are the signs?" That's what every woman wants to know. Are there signs that would expose the secret sex life of a down-low man? J.L. King and other authors have written that there are no signs. This statement is indicative of the narcissistic thinking of a down-low man who believes that just like he fooled every woman in his life to believe he is straight, he can also sucker women into believing that there are no telltale signs. Women who have been in relationships with down-low men have truly been given 20/20 hindsight. In this section, we will discuss signs that have been dis- covered by wives and girlfriends of down-low men, as well as signs given to us by down-low men themselves. These signs range from the most obvious to the very subtle. It is so important that you give all of the signs the same attention because what one woman may not recognize, another one will.

Intuition

The number one sign of detecting a down-low man is a woman's intuition. Webster defines intuition as, *"The capacity of the mind by which it immediately perceives the truth of things without reasoning or analysis."* Intuition has also been referred to as instinct, a sixth sense, a hunch, second-sight, and a gut feeling.

Our intuition speaks through fleeting thoughts, physical sensations, such as tingling of the skin, hair standing up on the back of the neck, and a bad feeling in the stomach. Others have described their intuition as a spoken whisper or an instant aversion to someone. It could be an uncomfortable feeling that something is weird, off, or wrong.

Janine's intuition made her feel that something was not quite "right" with Gary. She even asked him if he were gay and he lied and said no. While a woman's intuition may not specifically warn her of a down-low man, it is definitely a bonafide red flag telling her to steer clear of this relationship or at best, investigate further and get to know who this person really is. The fact that Janine even questioned whether Gary was gay was a bad indication and a cause for great concern.

Ladies, we don't give enough importance to our intuition and therefore, we ignore it or dismiss it as irrational or foolish, but God gave it to us to protect us. Our intuition often tells us what our brain and heart doesn't. Our brain says, "That's a fine man!!! Our heart says, "Its time to fall in love." But, our intuition says "RUN, RUN, RUN… he is not the one!"

Something else we often do is discount our intuition so that we can make the man fit into our lifelong fantasy of Prince Charming. When we receive red flags from our intuition, we're often afraid to ask the appropriate questions because we already know the answers will destroy the chances of our fantasy coming to life. What is it that makes us do this, ladies? Is it low self-esteem, emotional immaturity, lack of trust in ourselves, fear of being alone, fatherless homes, cheating brothers and friends, financial woes, or plain old desperation?

A desperate woman is the perfect cover for a down-low man. If you recall, Janine was just coming out of a relationship when Gary came disguised as her knight in shining armor. Janine did not give herself time to heal after her previous marriage failed, which set her up as a victim, thus she accepted the lie that he was not gay as truth without further investigation.

Janine's intuition acted like a lie detector right from the start. She was uneasy about Gary and as you recall, she asked him if he was on the down-low, but when he lied, she trusted *him* instead of her intuition. Even then, her intuition did not change *its* course and Janine went from a feeling of uneasiness to a state of depression that she couldn't understand. Our intuition is not a figment of our imagination, but really does reveal the truth about someone without our own reasoning or logic and we have to be willing to trust it.

Lack of Sexual Desire

Most healthy heterosexual men have a healthy sexual appetite. They would love to have sex almost every day if they could, as the male sexual appetite is generally stronger than the female. For generations, women have used the same excuses for refusing their man's sexual advances, for example, "I have a headache," "I'm on my period," and "I am just too tired." Sometimes a man will give excuses to his woman for not wanting sex at the moment, but this is not the norm. Ladies, beware if your man is giving an excuse almost every night, he may just be on the down-low. This is especially true if sex diminishes early in the relationship or marriage.

If a man has no physical or medical reason for his disinterest in sex, he may be attracted to men and cannot be aroused by a woman. This may be especially true if he refuses to seek help for his "supposed" erectile dysfunction. Lack of sexual desire may include no sexual arousal at all, loss of erection during sex, wanting oral sex only, and mechanical sex lacking passion. One wife of a down-low man described how her husband actually fell asleep during intercourse; another said her husband fell asleep numerous times. In each case, the wife thought it was her fault, thinking she wasn't sexy enough to hold her man's interest, especially since they only had sex four times during the entire year.

Some former down-low men, now totally out of the closet, explained how they had to fantasize about having sex with men in order to become aroused and maintain an erection for their women. Even though they may not admit it, in variations, this seems to be true in most down-low relationships. Some down-low men have been known to use Viagra, even though they are young and had no known medical reason for its use. We believe that they used it in order to obtain a medically-induced erection. Women in down-low relationships also related that their men liked to receive oral and give anal only, with no consideration at all for the woman's sexual satisfaction. Some women have related that their husbands have asked them to use strap-ons, dildos or butt plugs. These women also described how there was no passion, intimacy, or real affection in their everyday relationships. Another woman added her husband always wanted sex; however, the sex was so mechanical that she could clock his every move during intercourse for 25-plus years. She referred to it as intercourse instead of lovemaking because there was no kissing, fondling, or cuddling. There was no heart connection whatsoever. It was just mechanical, predictable, boring intercourse. Soon she found herself having to fantasize about other men in order to achieve any type of sexual gratification.

Many women unknowingly married to down-low men go for many years believing it is their fault for their husband's lack of sexual desire. They wonder, "Is it me?" "Am I too fat, unattractive, not sexy enough?" Their men often told them they were oversexed in order to shift the blame. These women suffered in silence, too embarrassed to tell anyone, even their closest friends. Women involved

with down-low men described that they felt neglected and insecure. They felt like Keisha—hurt and rejected. Imagine your man
telling you he is repulsed by your body and you having to beg him
for sex. Keisha is a very beautiful woman with a lot of sex appeal;
however, when we met her she walked with her head down and
shoulders slouched. These are two classic signs of low self-esteem.
No woman should have to take this type of abuse—and yes, it is
abuse. A woman deserves the love of a real man who adores her
softness, her smell, her gentle touch, her soft voice, and her caring
eyes—in essence, the very nature of a woman. She wants a man,
that when he sees her naked, blood rushes through his body
making his knees buckle. When a man sleeps with other men, he
cannot see his woman as that desirable person, because his sexual
stimuli are now perverted.

A down-low man is incapable of giving a woman all that is required
in a relationship, even sexually, because he is divided in his mind,
his body, and most importantly, in his soul. He is not able to create
the deep emotional bond that is very important in a committed
relationship, as his emotions are elsewhere. He is not capable of
experiencing closeness with his spouse; the sexual intimacy
required to experience "a one-ness" in his marriage, because his
wife is just a cover girl used to hide his true sexual desires. The
woman in a relationship with a down-low man is left feeling empty
and unloved. When she finally realizes the truth, she is left trauma-
tized, feeling like a fool.

Going to Gay Bars/Hanging Out With Gay Men

Ladies, repeat after me: heterosexual men do not go to gay bars, neither do they hang out with openly gay or effeminate men. Any
supposedly straight man who frequents gay bars is definitely a
down-low suspect. A straight man would not knowingly put himself into a position to be hit on and admired by gay men. You've
heard the saying, "Birds of a feather flock together." A straight man

seen in the vicinity of a gay bar runs the risk of being labeled homosexual. No true heterosexual man would be caught dead in this position.

Nadine's man not only went out to gay bars with Nadine's co-worker, but he actually befriended the man and was very comfortable with him. Most straight men go to bars to pick up women and/or to have a couple of drinks and shoot the breeze with the fellas. Why would a straight man choose a gay bar to go to when there are many more traditional bars available? Why? Because he *is* gay or curious!!!! Nadine, her man, and her gay co-worker went to the bar and did not leave until the bar closed at 6 o'clock the next morning. This should have been a major "down-low danger sign" for Nadine, but being the open-minded person she was, she thought it was all about dancing and having fun. She had no idea this was actually *her* man's stomping ground. He was very comfortable in the gay environment. Any man in a predominantly gay environment knows that he is fair game to be flirted with by the gay men around him. Many gay men prefer straight men anyway, and straight men know it. Gay bars are filled with men kissing, dancing suggestively and expressing sexual desire for each other. The sight of these open displays of homosexual affection is disgusting to heterosexual men. Many straight men would not dare to go see the movie *Brokeback Mountain* because they either had absolutely no interest in the subject matter or again they were afraid of being labeled as homosexual or at least curious.

The fact that Nadine's man hit it off so well with her openly gay co-worker was a bonafide red flag. Most straight men are nervous and uncomfortable around gay men and are too afraid that being seen hanging out with a gay man would tarnish their macho image. If your man hangs out with a buddy that is obviously gay, you should pay close attention because they just might be bed buddies.

Back in the day, if a woman's man had a good buddy that he hung out with a lot, no one thought anything of it, but in the society we live in today, a woman has to be very cognizant of everything around her. Heterosexual men love being with women, either their significant one or a few ladies they like to spend time with. Yes, they have buddies too, but their primary source of satisfaction is in the company of a lady. If you are in a committed relationship and your man's buddy seems to take up too much of his leisure time, and you feel uneasy or upset about it, don't just discount your feelings because he or someone tells you to. God gave you an innate instinct that will always be there for you. It will never let you down, but you must acknowledge and respect it in order for it to guide you in the right direction. Remember, Janine felt "catty" around specific male associates of her husband. Again, Ladies, let your instinct guide you here. Women know when another woman is trying to disrespect her and move in on her relationship with her man. Now that the down-low has been exposed she has to be aware of a new threat... her husband's male friends.

Gay Porn/Internet Activities

The Internet is a cyber-playground for men secretly leading a gay lifestyle and is especially helpful to the down-low man who needs anonymity. They are able to visit gay chatrooms, watch gay movies, surf gay websites and also place personal ads anonymously from the privacy of their homes. They are also able to send and receive e-mails from strange men complete with attached pictures. After reviewing the strangers' pictures, they can decide whether to hook up with one of them for a sexual encounter at a predetermined location. The Internet gives the 411 on the down-low parties given in their cities, where and when to be disclosed upon request.

While the Internet has made it easier for down-low men to operate, it has also made it easier for suspecting women to bust them. Ladies, if your man is secretive about his on-line activities, he probably has something to hide, and you need to find out exactly what it is. Call it snooping, jealous, silly, childlike... call it whatever you want, but if you are in a supposedly monogamous relationship you have every right to know if your partner is hooking up with men for sex. Your very life depends on it.

If your husband or boyfriend is always on the computer late at night, early in the morning or when you are not around, he may be hiding something. If he minimizes the screen or quickly closes the window when you walk into the room, then girlfriend, you need to do some snooping. If he's instant messaging and chatting with people you know nothing about, you need to make sure it's totally innocent and won't evolve into something that is detrimental to your health.

The first place to check on a computer is the Internet history. The history shows all of the Internet sites visited for a specific period of time. The easiest way to check the history is to hit "Control H" while in your Internet browser and the visited web sites will appear on the left. Also, under Internet options be sure to check the "cookies" folder. If your man is careful about covering his tracks, you can also buy a computer program that tracks everything that is done on your computer. There are many different inexpensive software packages developed for this purpose. Many record keystrokes and take pictures of the computer screen. You can also use it to obtain passwords to his e-mail accounts, chat rooms and porn sites. Some would label a woman a sneak, a snooper, dishonest, etc. If your partner is an upfront, honest guy, you would have no reason to be suspicious, but on the other hand if he shuns or ignores your questions, you need to investigate in order to protect yourself. Remember, some down-low men feel what you don't know won't hurt you and that couldn't be farther from the truth. Some down-low men also feel they are not cheating on their woman because they are having sex with a man instead of another woman. Regardless of his twisted reasoning, be informed about your relationship and act accordingly. Investigating may be the only way to find out the truth and protect yourself.

If you find out, like Keisha, that your man is visiting gay websites, it is almost certain that he is gay, curious, or on the down-low. A truly heterosexual man does not seek porn sites that are exclusive to gay men. Most straight men are repulsed by the sight of two men engaging in sex. When Keisha discovered what her husband was doing on the Internet, she knew for sure he was gay. He still denied it over and over again. To him, being on the down-low was not synonymous with being gay. So when she asked him, "Are you gay?" He answered emphatically, "No." She knew better. What would *you* think?

A woman told us that one night while visiting her new lover, she asked him to put on a porn video because he was having a little trouble getting aroused. He popped in the tape and there on the screen were two men having sex. She freaked and that was the end of that relationship. She knew then why he couldn't get an erection. Ladies, gay porn, in any form, is usually not entertaining to a straight man. Therefore, if you happen to see a gay magazine lying on the coffee table or hidden in a drawer, don't ignore it… ask questions or flee. Don't take chances with your own life—no matter how much you like him. If he knew it was there and didn't get rid of it, something is amiss.

Excessive Telephone Usage/Secret Telephone Habits

Women love to talk on the telephone. We can stay on the phone for hours and hours talking to our girlfriends about any and everything… children, jobs, food, etc., *solving all the world's problems.* We can always find something to talk about. A woman can spend all day with her girlfriend only to return home, call the same friend and talk for two more hours. Most men, on the other hand, do not like to talk on the telephone for long periods of time. They say what they have to say and hang up. Men use the telephone to arrange appointments, discuss specific problems and/or exchange short tidbits of news or information. Most heterosexual men do not have long telephone conversations unless they are romancing a new woman. Once the infatuation period is over, heterosexual men are over the "making love on the telephone" days and long phone conversations become a thing of the past.

On the flip side, some down-low men will talk on the phone for hours with their buddies, because those buddies are really lovers. Men in sexual relationships with each other have more to talk about; therefore they tend to stay on the phone longer than heterosexual men. One of Janine's warning signs was Gary's excessive use of his cell phone, especially during the times he was commuting to and from work. When Gary arrived home, he would often sit in the car and talk an additional twenty minutes before walking into the house. When Janine would ask him who he was talking to, Gary would often say it was his boss. Later, when checking the cell phone bills, Janine would find an unfamiliar phone number. In fact, every month, Gary had pages and pages of unfamiliar telephone numbers. When Janine called the numbers, unfamiliar men would answer and none of them were Gary's boss. Janine also heard telephone conversations between Gary and a man where he shared details of his life that he had not even bothered to share with her. As you can recall in Janine and Gary's story, Gary also became upset if Janine answered his cell phone. He allowed her to open his mail, but his cell phone was off limits. This was definitely a sign that Gary was hiding something from Janine. Gary would also turn his cell phone off during the times he was at home and would not turn it back on until he was backing out of the driveway the next morning.

If your man is secretive and ritualistic about his cell phone calls, he may be having a secret affair with someone, either a man or a woman. Examples of ritualistic behavior are: he always erases his messages right away; turns his phone off faithfully when he gets home; hides it or keeps it out of your immediate reach and only uses it when he is not in your presence. These things are planned and contrived not by just down-low men, but cheating men—period.

Men on the up and up don't plan phone usage, time-wise or other-wise, and traditionally only use the phone to make plans or when absolutely necessary.

Lack of Intimacy

Intimacy in a marriage/relationship means being able to share emotionally with your lover. This includes sharing your innermost thoughts, feelings, secrets, fears, and desires. Intimacy is achieved through allowing yourself to be vulnerable to another. It requires safety, trust, compassion, and empathy. In short, intimacy means being real with your partner on a level that is most likely much more intense than in any of your other relationships. It sets this relationship apart from all others. You feel secure because you feel that you are loved unconditionally. Having intimacy with your significant other is the most rewarding aspect of a relationship.

Intimacy is impossible in a relationship with a down-low man because he is not willing to be open and honest with his wife or girl-friend. True intimacy is nonexistent in that type of relationship. A down-low man will not share his true feelings with his woman because if he did, he would then expose himself. His very existence as a down-low man is that he dates women openly, but sleeps with men on the down-low. So, a woman in love with a down-low man really misses out on a true connection with him. While she is trying to get to know him better, he is getting better and better at manipu-lating her feelings and sooner or later, she is left heartbroken. We use the phrase "true intimacy" because a down-low man will try to give the illusion of intimacy. For example, he will share all of his childhood disappointments and triumphs. He'll tell you all about when, where, and how he grew up and who was in his life. He will share his accomplishments with you and he will also share his pain-ful memories. He will make you feel that you are the only one in the world he trusts with this information. Most women are nurturers and fall hook, line, and sinker, and are ready to be reeled in. Soon, the mate of a down-low man will begin to feel an emotional detachment from her partner, but she will fool herself by telling herself that he has shared everything with her. Janine felt lonely, insecure and insignificant, yet she didn't know why. Her marriage was not fulfilling because she felt no passion from her husband. The soft look in the eyes of a man when he loves, desires, and adores a woman is unmistakable. Yet, she couldn't remember ever seeing that look in his eyes. Whenever she asked him if he loved her, his mouth said, "Of course I do," but the expression of his eyes, said "Would you please shut-up and leave me alone."

Janine's down-low husband really wanted to be with a man so he was incapable of loving Janine the way she deserved to be loved. Gary was emotionally disconnected from the marriage, as well as from his wife. He showed no interest in her and avoided conversations with her. Intimacy requires open communication. Gary was really disconnected all along and soon began to show his real lack of concern for her. He did not show the normal, innate protective nature of a man who loves his wife and family. When Janine was falling apart under the weight of it all, he ignored her and turned away from her, often leaving the house while she cried hysterically. Even though he knew he was the source of her misery, still he treated her with a total lack of compassion. That old scripture of "the truth with make you free," comes to mind. Gary could have been truthful with Janine about his sexual escapades at anytime. He would have been free to be who he really was and at the same time allowing Janine to make her own choice, thus setting her free. True intimacy requires that deep level of honesty.

Constant Criticism/Abuse

This is one of the more difficult signs for us to write about. In Keisha's story, as soon as the honeymoon was over, Anthony began to criticize her housekeeping skills. Even though she was a neat person herself, he made it very clear to her that he didn't like seeing any of her toiletries, curling irons, pantyhose, or other personals around. Even the neatest straight man enjoys seeing his lady's personals in his environment once in a while. Anthony's dislike was so blatant that he seemed disgusted by the sight of Keisha's things. She felt belittled and insignificant, but she just told herself he was a neat freak. Her feelings were hurt and she felt uncomfortable in her own home, but she told herself things would get better with time.

Although Keisha had a nice figure, Anthony told her that her body repulsed him. Even the presence of his own daughter seemed to irritate him and he wouldn't even let their little girl play in the living room. He just seemed to be really annoyed when Keisha and their child were around. She couldn't do anything to please him. Soon she began to believe that the inadequacies he constantly pointed out in her were true.

Summer's man was also verbally abusive. He told her she had no eye for decorating and her homemaking skills left a lot to be desired. At first she thought he was being helpful, but he soon took over and made her feel he was the better housewife. He picked out the furniture, the wallpaper, the draperies, the paint color, the dishes, and other niceties. They argued constantly about decorations for the home because she felt this was her domain as the woman of the house. Unfortunately, other wives unwittingly married to down-low men have described the same abusive behavior. Their down-low husbands criticized their housekeeping, how they were raising the children, their cooking, their style of dress, and how they wore their hair. Sometimes instead of criticism, the men just ignored their women by never complimenting them. One woman talked about how her husband told her she needed to lose weight, but when she did, he never once mentioned it. Other women reported that the verbal abuse escalated to physical abuse, especially if they confronted their husbands about their confusing behavior. Down-low men often use the fear factor to scare their wives off, blaming them and accusing them of being insecure, nosy naggers. This tactic only lasts for a while and the wife may back off as her questions are left unanswered. We believe that the stress he feels from living a double life manifests as resentment, which turns into verbal, emotional and/or physical abuse toward the very partner he has tried so hard to deceive in order to keep his cover.

The women married to down-low husbands could do nothing to make their men happy. Why? Because a gay man is not content in a relationship with a woman and regardless of what she does, he will not be completely fulfilled. Some women with down-low men think that if they love them enough, they will change their abusive, controlling behavior. Unfortunately, their love is not enough and pretty soon the wife is just as unhappy and depressed as her husband. The women lose their confidence and self-worth and feel like empty shells because their emotional well-being has been compromised by neglect and abuse. Sometimes they turn the hurt inward and blame themselves for not being good enough.

The down-low guy has to bend or manipulate his woman's thoughts in order to spend time with his male lovers. Before long, she is totally controlled by him and his need to be deceptive. He will pick fights for no reason in order to get out of the house. Women have related times their husbands picked fights not just to *get out* of the house, but to *move out* of the house and shack-up with a man—unbeknownst to her—his lover. The down-low man is totally consumed with his desires and needs and will discount the emotional turmoil he is putting his wife or girlfriend through, because he cares far more for himself than he will ever care for her.

Ladies, it is so important that you make a decision to love yourself enough to keep your boundaries intact in your relationships. We will keep our boundaries with our relatives and girlfriends, but when it comes to our man, some of us throw caution to the wind and throw ourselves under the bus in order to keep that man happy. It is not just a matter of principle anymore. It is necessary for your very life.

Emotional Detachment

It has been determined over the years that the emotional health of a woman is vital in her love relationships because women are emotional beings. That emotional part of women allows us to love our children and husbands unconditionally. We will protect our children like mother bears protect their cubs. We will stand by our man during the good times and the bad. We love our families and will do whatever it takes to keep our families intact. Being women, we are raised to express our emotions through tears and conversation. On the other hand, boys are discouraged from showing their emotions. They are told to suck it up, don't cry. Even so, when a man takes a woman as his beloved wife, he should have a deep emotional connection with her. As the relationship progresses, he begins to distance himself ever so slightly from some of her concerns that he sees as "girly." Yet, when the going gets tough, he will be the first one at her side. He will be there to hold her and comfort her even if he does not understand the depth of her pain or even why it affects her that way. The bottom line is, he will try with all of his might to be there. In his book, *Woman Thou Art Loosed,* Bishop T.D. Jakes shares how he longed to be able to comfort his wife when her mother died. Even though he could not touch her pain, it hurt him to feel so useless to her. When a man is emotionally detached, he is indifferent to his wife's emotional distress call. He may not hear it or when he does, he chooses to ignore it.

One lady told us that while she was married for over 20 years, she could never figure out why her husband seemed to never be there for her when she went through hard times. She gave birth to their two children alone. She had about five surgeries in her life and couldn't forget waking up to an empty room every time. On one of those occasions, he didn't come to see her for two days and when he did, he was still in his party clothes. He came in apologizing with flowers in hand that were purchased for $5.00 at the corner store. He told her he had gone out with the guys. She had no idea that he really had been out with the guys—having sex with them. She wondered about the flushed red look of his light brown skin, but asked no questions. She was hurt and confused and tried to make sense of how a man who said he loved her and was supposed to be her protector and comforter, could be so cold and uncaring. She didn't realize until years later that he welcomed her hospital stays so he could plan sexual rendezvous with his male lovers, leaving her totally unsupported in her health issues. She felt very abandoned all through their marriage. For example, she spoke of his many unaccompanied vacations over the years. She complained to him that vacations were for families, but he seemed content on leaving her and the kids behind year after year. He would always go back to his hometown on these trips. She thought he even had another family back there. His family was large and they all loved her so when they said they knew of no other woman, she believed them. They were as perplexed as she was. It was later that she learned he was taking these vacations alone in order to have sex with men.

Ladies, if your man insists on taking vacations without you, that sexual urge to be with a man might be the reason. Whether you have children or not, vacations are for pleasurable, relaxing, fun time for you and the ones you love. Most people go on business trips or maybe to a funeral alone, but not vacations. This man made his wife feel she had to accept his going on vacations without her because they couldn't afford the extra expense. She accepted this early in the marriage although it hurt her every year. Near the end, his trips went from twice a year to three and four times a year. She thought he had another woman and was cheating on her, but he was always right there where he said he would be when she phoned him. His family never thought of another woman because he didn't display the traits of a man cheating with another woman. No women were calling the house for him and he didn't carry a cell phone. Of course, it never occurred to his family that the men that were calling were not just good old drinking buddies. Nor did it occur to the wives that the fishing, camping, or hunting trips their husbands said they attended with their buddies, were really not that at all. In this woman's case, her husband used fishing trips and even brought home fish, already dressed and cleaned.

A heterosexual man has a special quality we ladies love and that is his need to protect his woman and family. He will oppose any stranger or danger that threatens them. In a healthy heterosexual relationship, the man is so concerned with the physical safety of his family that he limits leaving them alone for days at a time. In today's world, men worry about intruders, burglars, rapists, and murderers and they would risk their own lives to protect their families from predators. No matter how big a fight he just had with you, he still feels like the terminator when it comes to protecting his woman. In Janine and Gary's story, once she found out about his secret life, it was as if a switch had been turned off and all "man of the house" behavior ceased. He began to even leave their brand new, beautiful home vulnerable to burglars by leaving the garage door open all night and not checking the locks on the doors before turning in for the night. His wife and children slept there, but he seemed almost oblivious to the danger to which he left them exposed. Could this have been out of spite?

Another woman told us that when a young man sexually assaulted their daughter, her husband didn't display the intense anger and rage most fathers would feel. Instead, she was the one that reacted. Her husband had a few words to say, but kept his distance from the situation. He didn't react in the usual way a protective father would. In fact, he didn't even try to comfort his daughter or wife.

That same woman talked of her down-low husband's strange way of hanging out with everyone other than her when they were in social settings. He would leave her sitting in one place, while he stood across the room or even in another room. She later realized that while she thought he was beckoning for other women's attention, it was really the men in the room that he was scoping out. She said whenever they walked into a club he would grab her hand and seemed to drag her into the room with a possessive arrogance, but then he would seat her and disappear into the men's room for the next 20–30 minutes. This happened almost every time. She talked of how strange men would walk up to the two of them and just begin talking to her husband. They would totally ignore her presence and he wouldn't bother to introduce her. She would call him on it after the man would walk away, asking why he would allow a man to disrespect her that way. He would act like he didn't know any better and would swear the next time he would react and not allow her to be ignored, but it happened again and again. These men were strangers to her—but not to her husband. They knew they didn't have to show her respect because they knew who her husband was and how he lived behind her back.

Nadine spoke of how her husband's friends were always hitting on her behind his back or giving her the eye. She would tell Gerome about it, but he would just shrug it off and say nothing, leaving her confused. She felt the man had no feelings at all. She never understood why he didn't confront his so-called friends. She later realized it was because they knew his secrets and knew they could disrespect him and his marriage and there was nothing he could do about it.

Down-low men also display their emotional detachment by putting the needs of others first. They will do for neighbors, strangers, their buddies, anybody else, cheerfully, while leaving their own women feeling neglected. Over the years of one woman's marriage, she described how her husband would come home and brag to her about how he had helped someone in a crisis and how proud of himself he would be. All she could think of was how he always refused to go out of his way for her. His lack of interest in things that affected her life left her feeling emotionally starved. People who knew them saw her husband as a very nice man, a man who seemed like a good husband and father, but behind closed doors he totally ignored her.

A woman, who we will call Betty, said she noticed that when they needed to replace basic necessities in their home like the wallpaper in the dining room or new towels and linen, her husband ignored her suggestions. But, when he would invite a bunch of men over to play poker or when family visited from out of town, he would even take out a loan in order to make those very replacements she had been asking for. He had to make others think he was a wonderful husband and father, when really he never gave to her from a cheerful heart. Emotionally, she felt disregarded and like a second-class citizen in her own home.

The experiences above are a just a few of the ways women have felt disregarded when involved with down-low men. Emotional detachment can be very subtle and slowly take its toll on a woman's self-esteem. One woman told of how, for such a long time, she never realized what an attractive woman she really was because her husband never told her or made her feel that she was sexy and beautiful. So when other men expressed their admiration or desire for her, she felt all they wanted was to get in her pants so she rebuffed them and gave them the hand to talk to. She didn't realize that she really was sexy and beautiful until years after her divorce when an old acquaintance told her how all the men he knew drooled over her and they still talked about her ten years later.

One woman went through more than 20 years of marriage with a down-low man and never once had a venereal disease, but the fallout of his secret life had ravaged her as a person. She looked in the mirror sometimes and wondered who she was because her self-worth had been slowly chipped away. One day he hated her, the next day he needed her. She lived in survival mode so much during their marriage that she didn't even realize she had ceased to live and just existed. Near the end of the marriage she became physically sick with chronic illnesses that she had never had before. She finally accepted the fact that the emotional abuse and neglect she had endured over the years had weakened her in every way. She had once been full of life, very intelligent, with goals of becoming a politician. She was vivacious and alive before she married him, but now didn't even know who she was anymore. The woman finally filed for divorce after many years, still not knowing what her husband was hiding from her. She divorced him because of all the horrible heartbreak his secret had put her through and finally, she was willing to give up loving him in order to save herself.

Shaving Body Hair

Shaving body hair is a natural part of a woman's grooming habits and has always been considered feminine. On the other hand, hairy chests, legs, armpits, and scrotums are natural for a man. Some down-low men shave their chests, legs, under their arms and most disappointing of all, their pubic hair. Shaving body hair has been a necessary part of some sports, but other than that, body hair removal is a trend that started in the gay community. We are still not sure why some men choose to shave their pubic hair, but it has been said that a trimmed or clean-shaven genital area gives the illusion of a larger penis. In the personal ads and profiles we listed earlier, a larger penis seems to be sought after and favored in the down-low community.

Even though Janine told her husband that shaving his body hair was a turn-off to her, Gary continued to shave in response to a gay-dictated preference. In many down-low ads, they often describe whether they are hairy or smooth and will request which of the two they prefer to hook-up with.

Other Warning Signs

The following warning signs are just as important as the ones discussed above; however, we felt these are more self-explanatory:

- Others tell you he is gay or you hear rumors that he is gay

- Frequently hangs out at the gym

- Difficulty making friends with straight men

- Molested as a child by another male

- Spent time in prison or extended time in jail

- Displays excessive hatred toward gays

- Checks out (watches) men instead of women

- Confesses to prior gay sex; however, he calls it experimentation and/or curiosity

- Wants a threesome with you and another man

- Admits to being bisexual (he is gay)

- Very secretive

- Never introduces you to the male friends he frequently talks about

- Still a virgin in his 30s, or has had limited relationships with women

- Always has a friend who needs help, but won't take you along

- Has an unusual interest in interior design

- Insults or makes fun of you in front of his male friends

- Washes his own underwear/frequently rinses them out by hand

- Always comments on how good-looking or well-dressed other men are

- Spends too much time in public restrooms

- Semen, fecal matter, lubricant and/or blood stains found in his underwear

- Has difficulty holding his bowel movements (possibly sphincter muscle damage from anal sex), resulting in accidents

- Men's clothing that shows up in your home or car that doesn't belong to him

- Buys personal gifts for men; for example, jewelry

- Has a picture of a man in his personal possession, in the wallet, on the mirror, as a screen saver, etc.

- Slips up by using lingo that gay men use

The signs above may not be portrayed by every man on the down-low and some down-low men will even portray signs not discussed here. In essence, we have given you guidelines to use in helping you find answers to questions your very own intuition has already brought to your attention. Please keep in mind that some straight men could also have one or two of the above signs. However, you must be your own judge in determining whether you should look further into your situation. Some signs may scream "down-low," such as gay porn, while others may be more subtle, like frequently hanging out at the gym. We are in no way giving your situation a critique. That is up to you.

Part Three

Taking Control of Your Life

Out of the Closet

If you suspect that your man is living on the down-low, there are several things you must do to protect yourself. We know you are feeling shocked, betrayed and devastated; however, you need to take immediate action to prevent this man from ruining your life any further.

First, you need to stop all sexual contact with him and anyone else. Continued sex with your man will only expose you and other future partners to sexually transmitted diseases, including HIV/AIDS. If you decide to continue sexual contact, please use protection. The majority of the women we spoke to were completely disgusted with the thought of having sex with their down-low men, but one woman still continues to sleep with her husband, even though he gave her an STD.

Second, go get tested for STDs as soon as possible. This includes HIV and all sexually transmitted diseases. Be sure to repeat your HIV test six months after your initial test. We cannot stress this enough—GO GET TESTED!! We know you are afraid, but it is better to find out sooner rather than later. Remember, Keisha's husband gave her chlamydia, Summer's man gave her gonorrhea, and although it is not in her story, Janine tearfully confessed that her husband also gave her an STD. We also spoke to two women (who did not want their stories published), who later learned that their husbands were HIV positive. Fortunately, both women tested negative. However, some women were not so lucky. Please, ladies, get tested and use protection in all of your future relationships. I am sure you have all seen the news stories of HIV-positive men purposely infecting unsuspecting women. One popular urban radio show had a program on air about down-low men. A gay listener called in and stated he was HIV positive, yet he continued to sleep with married men on the down-low. He confessed he probably had sex with as many as 60 married men since he tested HIV-positive. When the radio host asked him why he would do such a thing, he said something along the lines of, "Someone gave it to me and they didn't care, so why should I care about who I infect?" Scary, huh? But true, nevertheless. Ladies, get tested and use protection. We are in no way saying that you can only get infected with HIV or sexually transmitted diseases from down-low men, but your chances are higher because down-low men are sleeping with men as well as women, and therefore putting you at greater risk.

Third, make sure you are aware of your total financial situation, especially if you are married. Be sure to get copies of all bank statements and if you are planning to leave, you may want to transfer some of the funds into a private bank account that is in your name only. Also, be sure you have copies of all tax returns, house records, and business records. Make yourself familiar with your husband's retirement/pension plan and its impact on you in case of a divorce. Another thing to do is to cancel all joint credit cards immediately and open a credit card account in your name only. If you don't do this you will later find yourself paying for his fancy vacations, clothes, dates with his next cover girl, and you may find out you are paying for his new apartment with his male lover. He could also ruin your credit report, so contact all three credit bureaus, Transunion, Equifax, and Experian, if you're in the USA. Some on-line companies will provide you with an inexpensive compilation of all three credit bureaus' reports. If you are married and/or have children with this man, you need to consult with a lawyer immediately. Be sure to take all of your financial records and evidence of his down-low activities, such as private investigator reports, e-mails, gay porn site affiliations, pictures, letters, cell phone bills, etc., to your appointment with your attorney. Be sure to go online or consult with your attorney about the specific laws of your state. Some states recognize the devastation of adultery and compensate the victimized spouse by way of alimony and child support. Ladies, it is no longer acceptable for you to spend your time in a committed marriage and walk away with nothing.

We know this may sound overwhelming, especially in your fragile, emotional state, but this is necessary for your financial protection. Try to gather all of your financial information and change your accounts *prior to* confronting your man with your suspicion. We cannot stress the importance of this enough. Once you confront a down-low man, first he will deny everything, then he will treat you like something on the bottom of his shoe. Remember, we are telling you this from experience. You will cease to exist to him because you are no longer useful as his cover girl. Do not make the mistake of thinking he will be fair to you, because the break-up is his fault. The down-low man does not see it that way in his little twisted mind. To him, it is your fault for blowing his cover so you have to be punished. Women have told us horror stories about how they were ruined by down-low men.

> It was a slow, but steady descent and I never saw it coming. When my down-low husband decided I was no longer needed in his life, he began to slowly devour our savings and credit card accounts. I had no idea what was going on because he handled all of the outside bills, including our taxes. I always bought the food, clothing, toys and whatever else our children needed. I had taken on this responsibility as a way to assure my family's basic needs were met because early on in my marriage, I realized my husband was not a good provider and had this way of using our funds everywhere else but home. By the time he had served nearly 20 years in the air force, we bought our first dream house. It was all I ever wanted and more. I was totally in awe of this piece of heaven we owned. About one year into living there, my husband suddenly stopped paying the mortgage. At the time, the bank had such a unique and special relationship with

me that they tried everything to keep us from losing our home. One evening a very influential man was to come over for dinner to discuss our dilemma and offer his support. I cooked my best meal that day and waited with baited breath for him to arrive. My husband had been very quiet about the meeting, never strategizing with me or even discussing the upcoming meeting. About 20 minutes before the man was to arrive, I looked up and saw my husband walking out of the front door. I said, "Wait! Are you going to make it back in time?" He never spoke a word, just kept walking and didn't even look back. Needless to say, we lost our beautiful dream house.

We moved into a rental house that I hated. It was too small for all the things we had accumulated over the years and I knew it would never be home to me. About eight months after we moved in, he stopped paying the rent. Even though I have worked all my life in clerical positions, I never made enough money to maintain the entire household we had built together. My husband's way of fixing money problems was to borrow more. About this time, he suggested we file for bankruptcy. I was livid. I screamed, "Why would we do that?" He had no answer and ultimately, I refused to go through with it until a lawyer told me that in the state we lived in, if he filed without me, I would still be held responsible for all debts I was affiliated with. I was totally stuck.

We were evicted from the rental. The first time in my life ever—I was evicted. I couldn't believe what was happening. We moved into an even cheaper rental, but nothing really changed. He still paid the rent if and when he wanted to, even though he could afford it easily. If I asked what was happening to our money, I was ignored. A year later we ended up in bankruptcy court. When I was sitting in that courthouse hallway, everything seemed so surreal. About four of our creditors were there. I was sitting alone on a bench when they congregated around me. They were talking to each other as if I wasn't there. My husband's little brainless head was peeping over their shoulders. Then one man said, "Well, he says they are getting a divorce." The shock that hit me made me sick to my stomach. I replied, "Where did you get that from? We are not getting a divorce." They all looked at me with a blank stare. My husband would not make eye contact with me at all. I sat through the entire court proceedings in a total daze. I heard absolutely nothing that went on in that room. My mind was fixated on what I had just heard in that hallway.

On the way home, I sat in the car full of fear. I was so afraid that my whole world, as miserable as it was, was about to change, that I rode home in silence. About two days later, my husband was ironing a shirt when he told me we were going to move into our daughter's two-bedroom apartment. I emphatically refused and he shut the conversation down as usual. The next day, my daughter called. I said to her, "Honey, don't pay any attention to your dad, we are not moving in with you." She replied, "Mom, Dad said *you* are moving in with me and *he* is moving in with a male friend of his." My blood started pulsating in my veins so hard I thought I would pass out. When I confronted him, his reply was, "Well, my friend needs help so I thought I would be his roommate for a while." It was like I was living in an Alfred Hitchcock whodunnit. The next day trucks pulled up to pack up our furniture. When I saw them pull into the driveway, I got up off the couch, packed my clothes, grabbed my German shepherd and walked out the door for good.

I ended up in a one bedroom on the far side of town. That was ten years ago and now I live in a two-bedroom apartment with a relative. I owe the IRS; (he had handled the taxes all wrong too); I have no bank accounts; I have no 401-K; I started a business, and because of deep depression, I lost it too; and right now if you asked me to loan you $20 I couldn't do it."

Ladies, I am sure that when you read the story above, you thought, "How stupid could she be?" In this particular case, she had been in love with her husband for many years and basically grew up with him, hoping one day he would become that perfect husband. She made excuses for him in her own mind and protected him from the ridicule of others, when really she should have let him learn from hard knocks and maybe somewhere along the way, the truth would have revealed itself anyway. She was the kind of woman that held the family together, not knowing her husband was slowly trying to tear it apart.

Ladies, please don't let the story above be your story too. Follow the guidelines we have given you here. On your money is written, "In God We Trust." That means that you will pay attention to what is going on in your finances at all times. You will be diligent about protecting and securing your provisions. When you put your trust in your own God-given common sense, he will take care of you.

Janine, on the other hand, shared the following success story: "I found out about Gary on a Saturday evening. The first thing on Monday morning, I was at our bank when the doors opened. I withdrew the majority of our savings account and went to another bank and opened my own account. I felt better knowing I had enough money to rent my own place and support myself for the next few months. When we got married, Gary had awful credit, so I added his name to all of our credit card accounts. I immediately called all the credit card companies and had Gary's name removed from the accounts. A few weeks into my nightmare, I had the presence of mind to draw up a separation agreement giving myself the majority of our home's equity, stipulating that Gary had to pay half of all household bills until our home was sold. Gary refused at first, stating he wanted half of everything; however, he had a change of heart after receiving threats from my brothers. He reluctantly signed the agreement. Ladies, even if you have no brothers that will have your back, don't be afraid to stand on your own, as your state's laws will protect you. After our house was sold, I had enough money to start my life over. Yes, I was depressed and devastated, but I sure felt better knowing I was not financially ruined."

Fourth, reach out for emotional support. Do not isolate yourself out of embarrassment. You have nothing to be ashamed of. Talk to a trusted friend or family member and let them know what you are going through. They can help you get through this horrible ordeal. If you feel too ashamed to tell your family, talk to your religious leader or to a counselor. You need outside support to help you make the right decisions. There are many straight spouse networks on-line that can be of some assistance to you. Our experience has been that the down-low is very new to most of these self-help groups, but they too went through the tragedy of finding out their husbands were gay. You may feel so depressed that you may be tempted to walk away from everything, leaving all of your possessions to the down-low man. Your support system can keep you from making irrational, hasty decisions that will be detrimental to your future.

Last, but not least, take care of yourself. There is nothing wrong with taking medication if it is needed to help you cope. Let your family doctor or psychiatrist know what you are going through and discuss anti-depression medications if necessary. Try to eat healthy, exercise, and take vitamins, especially stress tablets. Exercise is good for releasing anger and is not only a natural way to reduce stress, but also depression. Another way to reduce stress is meditation and journaling your thoughts and feelings. Keeping a journal is an excellent way to cope and let out the pent-up anger. Please don't think the down-low man is going to let you vent your anger and emotions to him. He will be out the door quicker than Flash Gordon. You must find a way to let out your feelings, as some experts believe depression is nothing more than anger turned inward. Most importantly, pray to God for strength and guidance. All of the women we spoke to said they kept their sanity through God and prayer.

Emotional Roller-Coaster

After finding evidence of homosexual behavior, many women experience an odd feeling of relief mixed with shock. They knew something was wrong in the relationship and now they had a name for it. They now know the source of his anger and lack of sexual desire. It wasn't her after all, it was him all along. It wasn't her looks, her body, her cooking, her style of dress, etc., it was his secret sexual orientation—that he is in fact, a gay man. Janine described this initial sense of relief as "depression lifting from her body." She felt the relief as soon as she heard Gary's lover on the voicemail because she now knew the source of his discontent and her depression. The relief is short-lived, however, and soon other emotions take over.

Once the woman confronts the down-low man, she will go through a very painful roller-coaster ride of emotions. Through her shock, anger, and hurt, the first thing she will do is try to get the man to admit to his homosexual activities. This is extremely frustrating because she knows the truth, but he will still deny it, even when confronted with damning evidence, (e-mails, movies, letters, magazines, etc.). This will further add to the woman's anger because talking to the down-low man will make her feel as if she is talking to a brick wall. He will either deny it or not say a word at all. On top of that he will treat the woman as if it is all in her mind. She will think this man never cared for her at all and she will feel victimized and used. Anger will turn to rage and physical violence is very possible. Janine shares the following account of how her anger escalated.

"I tried and tried to get Gary to tell me the truth, but he totally ignored me. I watched every day as he went on with his life as if nothing had happened, while I slowly sunk into a black hole of despair. He even bought himself a new luxury SUV without consulting me. Gary moved his things into the guest room while I stayed in the master bedroom. One Sunday evening I decided to confront Gary one last time. I walked into the guest room where he was relaxing and talking on the phone. He looked at me and said, "Can't you knock?" At this point I snapped. I walked over to Gary and slapped him as hard as I could. I just had to wipe that smug look off of his face. Gary hung up the phone and called the police on me. The deputy came, but I was not arrested because I said Gary hit me first. The officer left and after packing a bag, so did Gary. He never moved back home and soon after, we divorced."

Rage is a very understandable emotion in this situation. The women of down-low men have been lied to, cheated on, exposed to disease, and used as covers. They face losing their homes, their life-styles, their jobs, and having to raise their children alone. They feel the burden of facing all of these issues while their down-low men behave as if they don't have a care in the world.

There is another emotion the woman feels, which others may not understand. Even the woman herself is confused by it. That emotion is sympathy. Yes, through all of the hurt, pain and devastation, she actually feels compassion for the down-low man. Why? Because even though she feels now that he never loved her, she actually loved him. When you truly love someone, it is very difficult to turn off your feelings even when the other person has hurt you. During this stage, the woman feels both sympathy and anger toward the down-low man. She wonders "Why is he gay?" "Was he raped or molested as a child?" She tells herself it must have been so horrible for him to live a lie. She tries to take the responsibility on herself and wonders what she can do to fix this. She even goes through brief periods of hope for the relationship.

Keisha and her husband felt they could pray his homosexuality away and they became more involved in their church. Janine tried to talk Gary into marriage counseling, but he refused. This is a very confusing time for the woman and that is why a support system is so important. Her emotions will alternate between despair, fear, anger, and hope. She may neglect her appearance and her children.

She will most likely isolate herself from other people. She may feel stupid for having compassion for the down-low man, and for not knowing the truth about him—especially if she was married to him for many years. She may feel humiliated and foolish because other people knew all along and were probably talking about her behind her back. At this point, she may self-medicate with alcohol and/or drugs—anything to escape the mental anguish. She may overeat, not eat at all, or engage in other self-destructive behavior. The casualties from the down-low are immense and tragic.

Through all the pain, some women reported frantically searching the Internet and library for any information on the down-low and gay lifestyle. Nadine said she probably read every article written about the down-low. Janine began surfing gay web sites to learn everything she could about the lifestyle. One day she asked Gary if he were a "top" or a "bottom." Gary appeared stunned that Janine even knew any gay lingo.

As the woman begins to understand more about the down-low, she knows in her heart that their relationship will never be the same. She has to make a decision about the marriage/relationship knowing that whatever she decides, her life will be forever changed.

Decision-Making Time

Basically, a woman involved in a relationship with a down-low man has only two options to choose from:

1. Stay with him and ask him to promise never to engage in homosexual activities again.

2. Leave him.

We are not advocating any one choice over the other, because we feel it is a personal decision. Only the woman can decide how she wants to live her life. However, we will discuss these choices in more detail and the ramifications of both. Keep in mind that we are speaking from our experience, as well as the personal accounts other women have shared.

Stay With Him: No More Down-Low Behavior

This choice requires a great deal of trust on the woman's part. Usually this is the first possibility a woman thinks of because she is sometimes still so very much in love and being without him is so foreign to her. Furthermore, she is asking herself to trust someone that has already proven to be untrustworthy. There are so many things she has to consider if she decides to stay in the relationship. The following are just a few questions that she needs to ask herself before making the decision to stay.

- When he leaves the house to run an errand, will she worry about what else he might be doing?

- If he begins to back away from having sex with her regularly, will she be able to deal with unsatisfying sex or no sex at all for the next 10 or 20 years? Will she constantly think he is fantasizing about men when he is having sex with her? When she has sex with him, will she constantly envision him having sex with men or be repulsed by his past sexual escapades?

- Can she be confident that he will not give her a sexually transmitted disease?

- Will she be able to handle the ebb and flow of her own emotions of worry, anger, and suspicion? How will she protect her own emotional health while she fights to keep this marriage/relationship together?

- Will she be capable of believing that he can be faithful? Can she really be confident that he loves her and is not staying just to keep using her as his cover girl or for monetary convenience?

- How will her staying affect the children in the long run?

- Will she be willing to compromise her own spiritual or value system in order to stay with this homosexual man? Will she consider the long-term effects?

- Will she honestly answer the question, "Why am I staying?" or will she choose to remain in denial, ignoring the questions in her own mind?

Even though the woman is receiving feedback from many sources in her social structure, i.e., pastor, parent, sibling, friend, or support group, the decision to stay has to be well thought out by her. Most women going through the down-low experience lose faith in their own decision-making abilities. They second-guess themselves, feeling their judgment is somehow flawed because they didn't see him for who he really was. Still, the decision has to be made by her because ultimately, she is the one who will have to live with the decision and the man.

Unfortunately from our research, the majority of women who decided to stay have reported that eventually their partners cheated again with men. Of the stories in this book, Keisha is the only woman who decided to stay with her husband. Every time we have spoken with Keisha, she sounds so confused and stressed out. Even though he promised her—and God—that he would not have another homosexual relationship, James has cheated with a man, yet again. One day when we spoke with Keisha, she was finally making plans to leave James, stating she had had enough and couldn't take it anymore. She said she had finally accepted the truth that her husband was gay and she was ready to move on. Two weeks later, Keisha informed us that she had changed her mind yet again.

Chances are the marriage or relationship will not last and years down the line when he decides to come out of the closet, where will that leave her? Women have to realize they have a future to consider. They must make their decisions based on their own needs and theirs alone.

Leave the Marriage/Relationship

Most women immediately make up their minds to leave the marriage as soon as they find evidence of down-low behavior. They are not willing to put their emotional and physical health on the line for an unfaithful down-low man. These women seem to have fared better and are able to move on with their lives much faster than those who try to stay. Women leave the marriage or relationship for many reasons. Here is how one woman explains her decision to leave:

> "This message is meant for any woman caught up in a relationship where the husband is described as having a down-low lifestyle.
>
> As a woman, I see no reason to stay with a man who lied and cheated. For me—for better or worse—does not mean he gets any sympathy from me when he's lied to me over and over again. When my ex and I married, we vowed to respect each other and keep our vows. That does not mean he gets to cheat with a man either, and

besides, I should have been told that his sexual orientation was homosexual. Had I known, I would NEVER have married him. If he didn't know he was gay when he married me, then as SOON AS HE FIGURED IT OUT HE SHOULD HAVE TOLD ME.

My ex betrayed me, lied to me, and caused me so much heartache. As a result, I will never trust another man again. That is the legacy he has left me. He took away my precious trust in men in general. Right now, the way I feel, I will suspect any man to be involved in the down-low lifestyle.

That is NOT MY LIFESTYLE. THOSE WERE HIS CHOICES AND I DID NOT AGREE TO THAT WHEN WE MARRIED.

Furthermore, a man who does that also exposes me to disease. Lying to me throughout the years tells me that my ex-husband IS NOT A MAN but a COWARD!!!!! I understand why my ex hid it from me but I'm still a human being who did not deserve to be lied to for so many years. I TRUSTED HIM 100 percent. NEVER FOR A MOMENT DID I QUESTION HIS INTEGRITY. I could have opted out of the marriage and have been given a chance at real love. Instead he is A LIAR, A PHONY, AND A FAKE.

My life will be lived happily WITHOUT A MAN!!! WHO NEEDS LIARS?! My take on this—any woman who would put up with this crap—is into abuse and co-dependency and is afraid to be on her own. It's a little like PROSTITUTION. You STAY WITH A MAN SO HE CAN TAKE CARE OF YOU. WHY NOT DIVORCE THE JERK AND MAKE HIM SUPPORT YOU AND GET PAYBACK FOR THE MISERABLE

MARRIAGE? How dishonest is it to stay in such a sham marriage. It is not an equal or healthy relationship when you are straight and your husband is gay. LET THE JERK GO! HE LIED TO YOU AND EXPOSED YOU TO DISEASE."

The feelings in the above message are shared by the majority of women we spoke with who were in relationships with down-low men. Many of them could not even comprehend the decision to stay in such a relationship. Specifically, the married women, because marriage and infidelity are not harmonious. The whole concept of marriage is to become one in a committed relationship. However, as previously stated, each woman has to make her own decision in her own time, in her own way, based on her own values and her own unique makeup.

Part Four

Up Close Comments From Down-Low Men

A Candid Interview

We felt this book would not be complete without presenting the viewpoint of an actual gay man living a double life. In the stories and experiences we have shared with you, we have given a voice to the disregarded, heart-wrenching truth about how the down-low shatters the lives of so many women. In expressing their anguish, the women have painted a picture of the down-low man as a cold-hearted, calculating, uncaring bastard. After all the heartache and anguish has subsided, the victimized women are still left wondering why and how this could have happened to them.

In an effort to provide some answers, we searched high and low for a down-low man courageous enough to give us an interview. The conversation below is entirely verbatim, only the names have been changed to ensure privacy. John (not his real name) will take you on a journey through his mind as he describes how living on the down-low complicates his life. His completely candid, honest depiction of his double life will answer many of your questions while at the same time will leave many unanswered. The questions asked in this interview are not merely the questions most often asked, but are the questions women were afraid to ask. John courageously agreed to do the interview because, in his own words he stated, "I will be entirely candid. I know full well that this is a complicated and heart-wrenching issue affecting many couples. Fear has ruled me most of my life. But I'm happy to help you out with this project. We all must search for the truth."

Are you still on the down-low or are you totally out now?
A few people know I'm gay—certainly the guys I have sex with know it. When I list myself online at personals sites I describe myself as gay. But I'm very discreet and virtually everyone I know in normal everyday life thinks I'm straight (I presume). So, no, I'm not "out."

Have you ever been in prison?

No.

When did you realize you were gay?

That's a tough one for me. I've resisted the awareness of it for so long—doubted it, rejected it, misinterpreted it, buried it, anything but faced it outright. I officially came out during a private therapy session nearly 20 years ago after 8 years of marriage. In some ways, though, I feel like I didn't fully realize that I am truly, inescapably, and undeniably gay until about 2 months ago, following a series of positive and satisfying homosexual experiences.

Were you molested as a child?

Not to my knowledge.

Prior to coming out were you attracted to both sexes and if so were you equally attracted?

I was always attracted to girls, even as a little kid. I made friends with girls more easily than other boys did, I think, and I wasn't as rough-and-tumble a boy as other guys were.

I remember taking baths when I was a young adolescent, maybe 12, and posing in front of the mirror naked, hiding my genitals and pretending I was a girl being ogled by and bid upon by boys. But my sense of it was that I wanted to *see* a naked girl, and I recognized that my young body wasn't that different from a girl's from certain viewpoints. Even though I was pretending I was a girl, I don't recall really wanting to be one. It's not clear to me what I was after; it's an old memory.

As a teenager, I speculated that perhaps everyone was really bisexual, and that most people chose the hetero lifestyle due to tradition, childrearing, social expectations, etc. I don't recall specifically why I thought that. Maybe I was just trying to be liberal-minded. In fact, there was not a single man or boy I had ever felt attracted to, while I found girls to be irresistibly pretty.

True, I didn't have a strong sense of masculinity. I was a quiet, pudgy, wimpy kid, into art and music and always the last to be chosen in team sports. (I don't know if the statistics support the familiar notion of homosexuality being caused by growing up with an absent father and domineering mother. I don't suppose they do, yet I did have a very close relationship with my mother, while my father had little involvement in my life.) But the idea of being gay never entered my head. I never felt attracted to any specific men—people I knew or celebrities. Still, I believed that, objectively, men could be attractive. That is, men aren't ugly, I reasoned, so why can't a man look at another man and acknowledge him as attractive?

I had no gay experiences during my teen years. Instead, I had been sexually active with girls since I was 15, even though I proved to be frequently—and quite embarrassingly—impotent. Perhaps being a 15-year-old boy and unable to achieve an erection every single time I was alone in the house and snuggled up in bed with a naked, buxom, and very enthusiastic 14-year-old girl should have been a clue to me. But what did I know? I thought I was just nervous. (To my deep regret, that girl did end up telling everybody I knew that I couldn't get hard, which I found painfully humiliating. In fact, the very next girl I dated eventually admitted to me that she had heard all about my inability to get an erection. It was no problem to her, however, since she was saving herself for marriage and didn't want to have sex yet.)

But I digress. As you may recall from my postings on the Gay Forum, I've always been more attracted to women than men, which has been a source of great confusion for me with respect to sexual orientation. Only lately have I tried to cultivate an attraction to men that I see, and my efforts seem to be working a little bit. But it still doesn't quite come naturally, whereas I can practically wreck the car when I'm at the wheel and happen to spot a pretty girl strolling along, just like any normal guy with an eye for the ladies.

With the help of that forum and my continued introspection, I'm becoming more comfortable with this apparent conflict. I find women to be very attractive; that's simply the way it is with me. I'm an inveterate girl-watcher. At the same time I do not have a strong desire to have sex with them or touch them in an erotic way. I used to as an adolescent, but no longer. I admire women for their beauty, but I crave men for sex.

I can enjoy straight porn—particularly with a fem/dom angle—as long as there are men involved. My eye always follows the naked man. (So many guys dig lesbian action, but not me. There's nothing more boring to me than two women going at it. Actually, I've always found it a little disgusting.)

Now this is a secret, which I've shared with very few people in my life—my wife *not* included—but part of my attraction and fascination with women manifests itself in cross-dressing—a secret fetish of mine for years. In the popular press it seems like cross-dressing is largely a heterosexual phenomenon, and no doubt it is. Heteros outnumber homos, so there are probably more straight cross-dressers than gay ones. But a lot of us gay men like the feeling of silk and nylon, and enjoy the rush of femininity one gets when wearing something soft and pretty.

Why did you get married?

I've been married to Lisa (not her real name) for over 25 years. At the time of our wedding I'd had only one brief, unsettling homosexual experience and did not consider myself to be gay. After drinking and flirting with an older gay man, he ended up partially undressing and groping me. I didn't stop him, but I froze up, and he stopped before long. So the issue had come up in my life, and I did find it confusing and troubling. The night of that experience, I thought that I must be gay. But by the next morning, it was as if it had never happened.

Before marrying Lisa, I had been engaged to my high school sweetheart, but we broke up after I met and fell in love with Lisa.

Now here's an odd part. Up till now, I've maintained that I didn't think I was gay before I got married. I still believe that. I also mentioned that I always struggled with impotence—the inability to get or sustain an erection, or difficulty achieving climax.

But in my college dorm room in bed with my attractive, naked fiancée, I finally thought I'd conquered my problem. How? By fantasizing about men—naked men. I'd keep those thoughts in reserve for when I wanted to get hard. Once I got going, I could be a long-lasting lover. When I thought it was time to climax, I'd let those thoughts of men back into my mind. Sometimes I even imagined that, somehow, *I* was the woman in the bed being penetrated by—I don't know—by *me*.

Yet, still, I didn't think I was gay. I had worked closely with a gay musician and felt frankly repulsed by the idea. These private thoughts I had were just dirty but exciting fantasies— and deeply secret ones. To me, for years, I thought of those gay fantasies as more of a private fetish than a true sexual orientation. I had, after all, only ever loved girls and women. I couldn't conceive of "falling in love" with a man. It seemed impossible.

Did you love her or was she used as a cover?
I absolutely loved my wife and still do, more than I've ever cared for anyone else in my life.

Did you try to change your sexual orientation? If so, why?

A gay friend of mine recently told me that he's never met a homo who would've chosen it over being straight. Why would anyone? It complicates life terribly. Being gay puts you in a small minority that is widely mocked and despised. Lesbians have it relatively easy; even straight men like to see women go at it together. Women in the army, in sports, and in traditionally male leadership positions are mostly admired. But for a man to be a little feminine—to even simply share a gentle kiss with another man—only provokes disgust or derision in most quarters.

But how do you change? I tried. I can't count the number of times I bundled up all my gay porn magazines and dildos and threw them away, determined to start afresh and no longer indulge in something that made me loathe myself. The last time I bought a dildo, it struck me that I'd bought these at least two or three times before only to throw them away, and then buy one again months or years later.

And why would someone choose an anal obsession in the first place? Though I feel an overwhelming need for anal penetration by a man and have come to enjoy it, there's no question that it can be painful. It's not nearly as easy and physically pleasurable as hetero intercourse. I admit it; intercourse with a woman physically feels better than anal intercourse with a man, giving or receiving. Yet I hope that I'll never have to have sex with a woman again, while I couldn't bear the thought of never again being taken by a man.

My method of fantasizing about men in order to have successful coitus with women was definitely an attempt to somehow change or at least redirect my orientation. I've spoken to other guys who also used the gay fantasy approach for this purpose. Imagine it the other way. What if a guy had to think about women in order to have sex with a man? Why would he bother? Why wouldn't he just be heterosexual and get it over with? That's what 90 percent of the world wants and expects.

I just came across some journaling I wrote in December 2005 in which I indicated my wish to be able to wave a wand or take some pills or therapy and finally become completely straight, free of all gay desires. It's only been within the last couple of months that I've finally freed myself from that hopeless wish. Now, every time I touch a man's hand, or feel his strong arms around me, or press my lips to his, the joy of it makes me glad I'm gay.

Do you have children and if so, do they know about your sexual orientation and how did they take it and how did you handle it?

I came out to my stepdaughter many years ago and she was fine with it. I don't know what she thinks today, considering that her mother and I are still together. I have a college-aged nephew who's openly gay, and I have several lovely nieces, but I've never come out to any of them, even my brave nephew.

Did your wife find out and if so how? Did you tell her, did she become suspicious, did one incident cause her suspicion? What were the circumstances surrounding your having to tell her or her finding out? What was her reaction?

About 17 years ago, after 8 years of marriage, my growing obsession with gay fantasies and desires left me with such low self-esteem and depression that I entered therapy. The therapist put me on Prozac, which I still take off and on to this day. I thought of it as my "anti-suicide pill" at the time and credit it with saving my life.

After two months I came out to my therapist. Within a week I told my wife. Lisa was stunned, taken completely by surprise. I believe it's true that she never suspected it. She cried a lot; she was angry and hurt. "Then our whole marriage has been a lie?" she'd cry, to which I'd say, "No, it's just that I changed over time from the person I was." Within a month we entered marriage counseling. Within six months, we separated. During that time I also came out to my brother, my step-daughter, and a few friends, all of whom were surprised, but supportive. I never did tell my parents. The separation lasted a year, after which we reconciled.

How did you feel toward her when she found out? Did you feel compassion for her?

I felt very guilty and certainly compassionate towards her. I had managed to "come out," but not proudly so. I didn't feel good about being gay. I didn't want it. Yet I did gradually feel resentful towards her about her bitter, emotional reaction. Sure, she was hurt; her life had been terribly upset. But I had been on the verge of suicide! I was struggling to face something in myself that horrified me. She was fighting for our marriage, but I felt like I was fighting for my life.

At the time a gay friend counseled me that Lisa only saw my predicament through her eyes, how it affected her life and self-image. He claimed that she would've probably preferred that I continue to bury the truth of my sexuality inside myself, no matter what the cost to my mental state, rather than be so selfish as to destroy our marriage. As he frankly put it, "She's not your friend." That statement haunts me to this day. To some degree, I think he was right—even though he didn't turn out to be much of a friend either.

Was the fear for yourself and your reputation more important to you than her emotional state?

Yes, definitely. How not? It may sound callous, but women are always in an emotional state about something. It's a mysterious and frustrating issue for men. Her weeping broke my heart at first, but as I tried to steel myself to it, to protect myself, I came to see it as manipulative on her part whether intentional or not. Eventually, her sorrow left me cold. That was my state of mind that preceded our separation.

Did you want to end the marriage? Did she want to end the marriage? Did you or she want to work it out and if so, what was your plan?

I guess I did, or thought I should. But neither of us were jumping at divorce. In spite of our sexual incompatibility, we had been enjoying a great relationship. So many friends and relatives looked upon us as some kind of ideal couple, based on our loving behavior towards each other. And it was true. We were like best friends—a mutual admiration society of two. Divorce never felt right, even if it seemed inevitable. In the end, a trial separation seemed like the best plan. It was to be an opportunity for me to "explore" and "sort things out," to "come to grips with this thing."

And I did explore to some extent, but really not much. I had brief, unsatisfying sexual relationships with only two men during that time, both gay friends whom I'd known for a couple years. Meanwhile money was tight. Lisa and I still shared a heavy debt load, and maintaining separate residences wiped us out financially for many years to come. During the separation, we both missed each other's company and telephoned each other frequently. It wasn't long before we started "dating." (She was fairly aggressive in this, trying to lure me back and restore our union. Friends she confided in at the time confirmed this to me later.) We also started having pretty good sex together again.

At the end of our separate apartments' leases, we elected to recommit and reunite. In all honesty, however, I had strong reservations that I have never shared with her. I know that, for her, it was all about love, marriage vows, etc. But a big part of my reason for getting back together was the money. I'm not sure she was aware of it, but we were nearly broke. I didn't see how we could go on living separately and still pay off all our debts. And since I'd made so little effort to be "out" and explore the gay life, I convinced myself that I probably wasn't really gay anyway.

Describe the atmosphere of your home after your secret was revealed or exposed.

Tense, certainly. Strained. She frequently opted to sleep on the couch instead of in bed with me, which hurt my feelings. Marriage counseling was supposed to help, though it only steered us in the direction of a separation.

Let's talk about the way you hid your double-life from her. What were the secrets you had to keep in order to keep the bigger secret; i.e. post-office box, secret cell phone, e-mail account she didn't know about, secret hobbies geared toward your down-low experience, for example, the gym, poker games with the guys, fishing trips or extra business trips, etc?

Fast forward 17 years. We're still together in a now sexless marriage. My homosexuality never stopped tormenting me, though I have long been able to keep it at bay through concentration on my work, masturbation with gay pornography, and increasingly heavy drinking. After a four-year stretch of celibacy (not counting masturbation) I found it hard to concentrate clearly on anything. I felt depressed about my life and maddeningly desperate for a man's touch.

The Internet makes hook-ups much more possible. In the past my only choice had been to go to gay bars in the hopes of a pick-up, later telling Lisa that I'd been out for a drink after work with the guys. Now you can skip the in-person small talk and make arrangements on-line. (And hiding porn and private contacts on one's computer is fairly easy, especially if one's partner isn't particularly computer savvy.) The Internet is an absolute boon to extramarital activities. Cell phones, too. Everybody used to have just one land line and one answering machine per household. Now, separate phone accounts are commonplace.

Did you ever bring your lovers around her and introduce them as a friend?

No, but I did have sex with two gay men who were friends of us both. In one case, it became a brief affair, which ended up ruining our friendship. Lisa knows that we no longer see "Brian" because he was in love with me. She probably figures that he and I had some sexual contact—he may have even told her for all I know—but she never asked me about it.

What kind of lies did you have to tell in order to get out of the house?

I never had a good method for getting out at night or on weekends, which limited my extramarital activities to the late afternoon after work. My excuse for being late was always either, "I went out for a drink after work," or "I had to work late." I also took advantage of every opportunity I could on those occasions when she went out shopping or on a business trip or whatever.

But my activities were really few and far between, spread out as they were over the course of several years, so it was never too noticeable. Lying to your wife—even when it's brief, simple and unquestioned—is disturbing, a killing of your soul, inch by inch. It passes quickly and you move on. At the time, it seems like there's no other choice.

When you made love to your wife, did you enjoy it, or was it a chore?

I enjoyed it at first, even though sex was always a struggle for me.

Did you have to fantasize?

I could get turned on by her looks, her kiss, or her touch, or by something sexy she wore—very much so, in fact, during the first years of our marriage. But most of the time I had to think about men in order to get hard and then later to ejaculate.

Did you have sex with her on a regular basis?

Definitely not. I used to fret about it when I'd realize we hadn't had sex for a couple weeks. I knew that soon she'd be cuddling up next to me in bed expecting something to happen. I'd plan to try to make love on a given night so that I'd be off the hook for a while, but it was hard to get myself to do it. I was always relieved whenever I was sick. I'd think, well, the one good thing about this flu is that she can't expect me to have sex.

Did she have to beg you for sex?

Sort of. She'd whine about it sometimes. She definitely initiated it far more than I ever did.

Was there passion for her as you made love to her or was it contrived?

We had a passionate relationship at first, particularly before we married. Afterwards we became less and less passionate, as most couples do with time and familiarity, I suppose. As I mentioned before, I had learned to function in bed with a woman by thinking about men, but that became harder and harder to pull off. Gradually it just depressed me when I'd feel her press against my back and put her arm around me. I'd feel her breasts and her soft skin, and I just ached for it to be a sensation of muscle and body hair instead, the roughness and heat of a man holding me, wanting me. I was finally satisfied to let her think I had erectile dysfunction; that I was impotent, rather than admit my unabated hunger for a man's attentions.

Did you have to fantasize about men to enjoy sex with her?

Fantasy about gay sex was crucial. But fantasy is still an important factor in good sex for me. Even when I'm with a guy, I often fantasize—just not about women.

Did you have romantic feelings toward your wife or did you have to role-play?

I had and even still have romantic feelings towards her, but I've never linked romance with sex as much as she does. Feeling love and romance is very significant to her when it comes to sex, as if sex were an expression of love. I don't quite see it that way. Sex is sex. It isn't about love; it's about passion, animal desire, orgasm. Love can certainly heighten the ecstasy, but I don't think it's required for good sex. It's a separate thing from romantic love. I think this is something that will always divide Lisa and me.

What were your true feelings toward her?

Love, regret, pity.

Did you have to compensate with material things to keep her satisfied in order to keep her in the dark?

No, we're not materialistic people. We enjoy each other's minds—our wit, our talents, our politics, our humor. We're also very co-dependent, indulging each other in our weaknesses and vices.

Did you feel any animosity toward her because you couldn't live your own truth? What kinds of jealousy, if any, did you feel—for example did you feel jealous when she was the object of men's desires instead of you?

On the contrary, I would love it if she took a lover to bed. I want her to have the sex life that she deserves and that I can't deliver. I admire couples who take part in the swingers' community, and I find cuckolding fantasies extremely exciting. I've hinted at this in the past, but she's never gone for it. She usually resents it when a guy flirts with her and seems to only want such attention from me.

As for animosity towards her, I admit it's there. It's very weak of me to acknowledge it, but I've often wished she'd demand a divorce. She's always been the more dominant force in our relationship, the decision-maker. Why didn't she ever make this decision for me? Just kick me out of her bed and out of her life? But that's lame, trying to avoid responsibility for my own life, looking for some easier way out of my problems.

Did men disrespect you in her presence, if so, why?

I'm not sure I understand the question. I can't think of an example of that, so I'll say no. Now, have I ever felt inferior and inadequate in comparison to other men? Absolutely. But that has to do with my self-perception rather than any way another man has behaved towards me.

Where did you go to meet men?

Gay bars, at first. Then a rather sleazy gay movie house with a glory-hole maze upstairs. In the last few years I started going to gay bathhouses. There are at least two in town here. Lately, however, I meet men at their place or a hotel after making arrangements on-line.

Did you have anonymous sex?

Yes, a few times. I found it unnerving and even traumatic at first, but you get used to it.

Did you consider yourself promiscuous?

No. I've only had ten or so gay partners over the course of nearly 20 years.

Did you have protected sex 100 percent of the time?

No, but most of the time.

Did you ever have sex with a man and your wife in the same day?
Only once.

If you did, what was your reason? Were you trying to recapture your feelings of masculinity or was it obligation?
That happened many years ago when I first came out. Releasing and indulging my gay sexual desire made me feel very potent and randy. During the initial coming-out period, I had some of my best sex ever with Lisa. I'm not sure why. As I said, I felt more sexually charged up than ever before in my life, and I really indulged myself.

How did you meet the men?
In bars... I tended to be bashful, waiting for someone, anyone, to speak to me, and I had to drink a lot to loosen up enough to even meet someone's eye. Hook-ups rarely occurred. At bathhouses you don't have to speak; it's much more straightforward. You might exchange a word or two, or just a glance. Then you just start going at it. Online, of course, you can exchange email, read people's profiles, see photos, and break the ice that way.

Did you ever have group sex and was that your preference?
I had sex as part of a threesome at a bathhouse last year. That was my first multiple partner scene and it was intensely pleasurable. I felt proud of myself for doing it. I like the idea of multiple partners, including larger groups, and I'm sure I'll do it again.

Did you attend down-low parties?
No, but I looked into it. I tried to join a "hotel orgy" group that advertises itself online. But I could never arrange to pull it off discreetly and finally looked elsewhere for opportunities.

Was there really a certain look passed between two men and if so what was that look? Was it a gaze that lasted more than a second, a wink, a nod?

Not that I'm aware of. At a bathhouse, if someone looks at you and you smile or even simply don't look away, that's enough.

How could you tell when a man was on the down-low?

I've only ever tried to hook up with a guy in an environment where I knew the guys around me were gay, like a gay bar, website, or bathhouse. I wouldn't dream of coming on to a guy out in the regular, straight world. Way too risky. I can't possibly tell if someone is gay just by a look or a "feeling" or something. Veteran queers talk about having "gaydar," but I have no experience of that.

Did you ever have sex with a man while your wife was in the vicinity, like maybe at a party, a department store, in the same hotel?

No, but I did flirt with a gay friend while we were at a birthday party for my wife. I was pretty drunk and, afterwards, mortified by what I'd said to him. Fortunately he was drunk, too, and never mentioned it. I still fantasize about him though.

Did you ever hook-up during your lunch break.

No, unfortunately, but it's a good idea. That was how the hotel orgy group was supposed to work. It seemed promising, but something always interfered with my plans.

How did being on the down-low affect your spirituality?

I'm an atheist and not very spiritual. I grew up in the church but cast aside my faith long ago. Being religious might have made it easier for me to fight off my gay demons, but I'll never know for sure.

That reminds me of something a therapist once told me. It was my first therapist, the one I initially came out to 20 years ago. (I posted this memory on the Gay Forum website, so you may recall it if you read all my posts.) I asked him what I should do, and he said I had three basic choices: either come out and live as an openly gay man; struggle to keep suppressing, denying, and channeling my desires away from it—noting that it would help if I had some religious conviction to back me up on that; or else I could continue to lead a double life, secretly arranging gay encounters with strangers while lying to my wife, family, and friends.

I remember thinking, at the time, that only the first two choices seemed possible at all, and only the first one was reasonable, since suppression of desire would be difficult without an anti-gay religious belief system to bolster me. The third choice—continuing the maddening, false-faced lifestyle that had driven me close to suicide and into therapy in the first place—was impossible; unimaginable. That one was out, I was sure of that. I felt certain that I would rather kill myself than go on as I had been.

Now, to my amazement 20 years later, I continue to live with that rotten third choice—the worst choice of all, but the only one I could bring myself to do. I do feel great shame about it. Not shame about being gay—not anymore—but shame about my cowardice and dishonesty. Yet, thanks to those ignoble choices, I have both things I wanted: my marriage, my home, a reputation as a straight, married man on one side and occasional anal and oral sex with men along with a secret horde of gay pornography on the other. The problem is that I'm incomplete in both worlds: my marriage isn't happy anymore, and the gay world is passing me by.

Did you have sexual encounters with men you met in church? Did any of your partners include ministers?

One was an organist (no pun intended) but, otherwise, no. He'd been aware of his homosexuality as a young teen. When I knew him as an adult, he used to joke about all these priests molesting choirboys that you hear about, and how bitterly disappointed he was that no priest had ever molested him! I know that sounds terrible, but it was funny when he said it. I guess you had to be there.

How did the down-low affect your emotions? How did you feel about yourself?

I never found it fun to lead a double life, and I've hated lying to my wife. I guess not enough, however, to stop doing it. I've always justified it by thinking that I'm sparing her feelings, that I'll be the one to suffer in silence so she won't get hurt. Noble of me, right?

Were you depressed?

Deeply depressed. In my early 30s, right before I first came out, I was truly suicidal.

Remember, our down-low men totally hid their emotional selves from us on every level. So please tell us how you were really feeling. If you felt nothing and had to compartmentalize your feelings, we want to know. Did you ever hate yourself; if so why?

My self-loathing came at me from several directions: lying to my wife and the world; having gay obsessions, which I saw as unmanly; not being the man I always hoped I would be; being afraid to come out when so many gay men live openly. These days, however, it's the lying that gets to me, the false face I present to my wife, friends, family, and colleagues every day.

If you fell in love with a man during your marriage, how did you keep your love affair completely undercover?

I am yet to fall in love with a man. I have only ever loved women. But at least I finally can *imagine* truly loving a man. I had to learn to feel good about being gay first. Now the idea of falling in love with a man—of being tender, vulnerable, sweet and romantic—seems very beautiful and extremely exciting to me. If I ever do fall in love with someone, I know that will spell the end for my marriage to Lisa. But I'm not out there looking for love. Just sex.

Not that I don't mind when there's at least a little romance attached to it. Of my two current boyfriends, one of them is a bit of a romantic himself. We're usually together in a hotel room for two or three hours every other week, and we do everything oral and anal we can think of during that time, but mostly we kiss. I've kissed him more in the past month than I've kissed my wife in the past ten years.

How many male lovers do you think you've had?

I'm not sure how to define "lovers." I guess I'd say I've had sexual encounters with around 12 men, 5 of whom I'd rank as lovers. A less romantic term is "fuck buddies," and that's really more appropriate, especially to describe the two guys I've been seeing for sex lately (one of whom is married).

Did any of them threaten to tell your wife if you refused to leave her?

Nope.

John's account of his life on the down-low depicted a mindset we found common to a lot of down-low men. As honest as John was with us, his initial dishonesty with his wife left her in great pain.

Coming Clean

Below is another story of a former down-low man who took the road less traveled and decided to honor his wife by being honest and coming clean about his lifestyle:

"I'm 51, the father of the greatest kids on earth and proud to finally say that "I am gay." It took years, maybe a lifetime, to get to this point but I'm happy for where I am and I'm proud of the way I got here.

Here's my story…

I had the perfect life that everyone wants. A terrific wife, great kids, the big house, the good job, the nice car. I had worked hard to get to where I was but I didn't do it alone. My wife was right there beside me all the way. Supportive. Attentive. Never a complaint. Happy to take a backseat to me and my career for the good of our family. A great person who was liked by everyone and to whom I was fortunate enough to marry. But, it was all to change.

To step back a few decades… I had a minor sexual encounter with another boy when I was 12 but discounted it as normal experimentation. I did, though, struggle somewhat over the years with my sexuality but only in fleeting moments. Growing up, I always had girlfriends and had satisfying relationships with them. More importantly, my wife and I had a great relationship for more than 22 years. And it was good in all ways. The sex was good. Often it was great. We communicated well and we stood by each other through good and bad. Neither one of us ever had an affair. I, did, though, have attractions to other men from time to time; but never once during those years did I ever act upon them. In reality, from the age of

12 until I was 48, I never had a sexual relationship with another man. Probably hard to believe but very true. I wouldn't allow myself to give in to the temptations because of my wife and kids.

The change came when I came very close to death due to a serious and sudden illness. After having had extensive surgery with a long recuperation period, I had a lot of time to think. I realized that my "urges" were more than that and now I wanted to act upon them. Eventually I did. I did the bookstore thing like the rest of us. But, I never had sex in the woods, at truck stops, in restrooms or any of the many other places that men often have anonymous sex. I was, though, just as self-absorbed in the conquest as the guys in the woods and certainly no better than them.

During and after my illness, my wife and I never had sex again. First, I recognized that I no longer had the desire to have heterosexual sex. Was it some epiphany that occurred as a result of the operation? I don't know, but something had changed. Maybe it was the recognition of how short life can be. I was still physically able to have sex with her and could have done it. No one would have ever known the difference (except me). But there was something more important to me. My wife. I knew that what I was doing in secret was wrong and I also knew that, because of it, there might be risk to her. Although I had not taken any serious health risks, I still wasn't about to have her unknowingly take any risks with me. I loved her too much and owed her more than that.

After some time of living another life, I decided that I could no longer deceive myself, my wife, my kids or anyone else that I loved (or who loved me). I was gay. I knew it; I accepted it and I didn't want to hide it. I wanted to deal with it in the best way I could. Maybe it would be the right way and maybe it wouldn't. All I knew is that I had to do something. I didn't HAVE to come out. I wasn't caught with someone. I wasn't caught looking at gay porn on the internet. I just couldn't be anyone but who I was. An honest guy with a conscience. Through the lies, I recognized that I wasn't being me and it tore me up. I knew that telling the truth was the best thing for all of us. After all, I deserved to be happy and so did my wife. Living the rest of her life with a gay husband wasn't an option in my mind or I'm sure in hers. She needed to move on with her life and find the happiness she deserved.

I came out to a close friend first. It was a little difficult but it was a very positive experience. I truly believed that what I was doing was the right thing and it made it all so much easier. I came out to my wife a short time later. Bear in mind, there had been no sex between us for quite awhile now. Just a lot of excuses as to why we weren't having sex. Eventually, I think we both came to the conclusion that neither one of us cared about having sex anymore. I don't think it bothered her much but we both knew that the emotional bond was breaking down because of it and things weren't heading in the right place any longer. When I told her, I explained to her that I could no longer live with the thoughts that she might be blaming herself for the lack of sex in our marriage. Maybe she wasn't pretty enough (she was) or thin enough (she was) or any other thing a person may conjure up in their head because of lack of affection and intimacy. It was never her and it wasn't fair that she might be thinking it was her. It was me. And, very simply, it was because I was gay. There was no room for interpretation. No other reasons. No other excuses.

She was shocked at first and hadn't suspected it. There were a few tears but not many. There were more tears on my part because I was so relieved that I told her and had begun a journey that I knew I could not and didn't want to step back from. But there wasn't any yelling or screaming. Actually, she hugged me and showed a true sense of support and compassion for me. She knew how difficult it was for me to do this and that the road ahead wouldn't be easy. I told her I'd always love her. I also told her that the years we spent together were never a lie and that I did love her emotionally and romantically. There were no fantasies of other men when we had sex. It was, for a very long time, the real thing and I had no regrets for the years we spent together, nor would I have changed them.

We recognized that it was time to move on and our lives were going nowhere in the meantime. What followed next was telling the rest of the world. The hardest part for me was my kids. Although I thought they'd be understanding, because they had been raised to accept differences in people and lifestyles, I wasn't sure how they'd feel about it being their Dad. They took the news extremely well. All of us cried, though. Not because of my sexuality, but because of the impending divorce, which we discussed with them at the same time. They were more shocked and saddened by the divorce because our relationship had been so good in so many ways, and yet it had been so bad in other ways that they couldn't see. From that point on, I haven't looked back and neither has my (now ex) wife. We have accepted this and have both begun to build new lives. My kids, my friends and my family remain my biggest supporters. Life is good, my conscience is clear and I'm finally complete.

I think much of the success around this was how it was presented. How I presented it to my wife. How the two of us presented it together to the kids and so on. Again, I didn't HAVE to come out to anyone. I could have gone on living a secret life but it just wasn't an option for me. And it certainly was not fair to my wife. To this day, we remain the best of friends. She'll always be a part of my past, present and future. I like to think that she is proud of me for what I chose to do and why I chose to do it. I hope she sees that it wasn't just for me. It was for me, for her, the kids and everyone else that needed to know the truth. As I told my kids when I came out to them, "I'm still the same Dad. You just know me a little better now."

I hope that sharing my story helps others out there to see that we need to find the courage to be ourselves, without shame. And we have a responsibility to do the right thing. Living the lie doesn't make us feel good about ourselves and it can destroy the lives of the people we love most. I wasn't willing to take that chance... "

Part Five

Updates From the Women Who Spoke Out

"Janine's Fairy Tale"

Janine & Gary

Gary and I divorced nine months after I discovered his secret down-low lifestyle. We sold our dream home and my son and I moved into a townhouse. I decided to remain on the east coast until he graduated from high school. I returned to work only to have to take off again on extended leave. It turns out the antidepressants prescribed to me had severe withdrawal side effects. Even two years later, I still suffer from fallout from my ex-husband's betrayal. The depression was so severe that it took many trials of different medications and in the midst of the trials, one medication was harmful to me. I still have not returned to work due to my medical condition. As for Gary, he is still lying and deceiving other women. The last I heard, he was dating a 21-year-old woman with a young child. I made a decision to have no contact with him in any form and therefore I have found peace.

Despite my distrust in men and my downright lack of faith in love, it happened anyway. Nine months after my divorce, in the form of a friendly, smiling face, my true soul mate emerged. I had known Daryl for months, as he worked where I shopped. He was always kind and personable and we made small talk, but he made no advances. When I mentioned that I was going home to visit family, Daryl finally let me know that he was interested in me. He told me to please come back because I would be coming back to him. When I returned, sure enough, this man was waiting for me. When I came into the store, I could hear his co-workers saying, "There she is." Soon enough, Daryl came from his office with a big smile on his face. He walked over to me with a look in his eye that I could not deny and handed me a card. On the card was his full name, home phone, cell phone, e-mail and home address. This was a definite first. It was as if the man could read my mind and knew that I was afraid to trust any man again. He asked me to lunch that day, still being cautious and tender with me. I accepted and since then we have been inseparable. One day in conversation, Daryl became very serious and said to me he wanted me to know God had told him that I was his wife and he should not let me get away. I was stunned and still skeptical. He told me if I didn't believe it, then I should ask God myself.

Well, I prayed to God and he answered me. A few weeks later Daryl called and asked if he could stop by after work. I said, "Sure." He walked into the foyer of my house and immediately whispered to my son, "May I have your mother's hand in marriage? You are the man of this house and I respect that and therefore I am asking you for her hand." I saw a huge smile cross my son's face. Daryl then turned to me and went down on one knee, opening that little box, most women want to see one day. Needless to say, I said 'yes'. We were married in a beautiful wedding chapel four months later. We have since bought a new home together and he has lived up to every promise he made me. I have already met and love his family and friends and I have to say I have never before felt the kind of security, love, and adoration this man of God has given me.

"Shattered"

Summer & Kenneth

Well, my life has gotten better. I finished school with a networking degree in information systems. I have been on a few dates, but I look at men in a different light. I used to wonder if every man I met was suspect, but I am slowly growing. I no longer miss my ex. I also no longer hate him. I have no feelings of love for him anymore. I am at the stage where I kind of pity him because a man that has to hide himself has to be in a lot of pain. I still coach my girl's track team and they are doing really well. I have met a man that seems to be good for me, but I am taking it slow with him. He knows that I am celibate and he does not pressure me. I do understand that this all will fall in place if God wants it to. I no longer wait for a good man. I only wait on God!

One week before this book went into publication, Summer received an email from Kenneth. Finally, after 22 years, he wrote:

> *"Summer, i hope this e-mail finds you in good health. I am trying to purge myself of some demons. First and foremost, you were right about me. I have known that there were some things about me that was strange at a young age. I tried to fight it. I however cannot openly admit it to you but you were right. When we first met i fell in love with you. You were my wife. I loved that little girl with the hardcore exterior with a heart of gold. I used to watch you tell all the fellas "no thanks but i got a man". I was so proud. When you had our son i was in awe of you!!! You handled the pain. But later on the feelings for my secret life came back. I slept with any and every woman i could*

to tell myself i was a man. You found out and left me. I knew i hurt you bad. The second time we found each other was a hope at a second chance. I thought i could fully commit. I bought you any and every thing i could to make you happy. We did everything together. When you made love to me i new you were mine only. You were always a fireball in that department. But my old life creeped up once again. You put up with me for 5 years and stuck by me. But when you found out it was not a woman i was cheating with you could not handle who that person really was. I watched as the tears fell from your face and you tried to be strong but i knew i had lost you forever. I miss you and when i came to your house last month you were friendly but you would not bend. I hope you have forgiven me for who i am. I owed you total honesty. In my heart you will always be my wife. But i notice that there is a sadness in you that won't go away. Baby i want you to be happy. Don't let what i did spoil things for the next man. I know it will take a long time for you to heal and i hate i caused it. I know your daughter's father still loves you but you won't give him a chance. I agree with you on that. He hurt you too. Don't be with a man that has brought you pain. We somehow never grow up. I want to ask you to forgive me. You told me you are celibate. I can't say that i am sad about that. I am glad no one else is touching you. But one day you will find that right man and give yourself to him. Until then wait until you feel ready. Please forgive me. I am so sorry. I am still going to keep sending the allotment checks to you. I owe you that much!!!! Baby be happy and i will always love you!!!!!!!!!!

LOVE,

Kenneth"

"Southern Comfort"

Saundra & James

Well, my friends, since last talking with you a year ago, I went into the hospital with a Lupus episode that took me on a two-week excursion. For a moment it was pretty tricky there; however I did recover and for the first time in a long time I weigh over 130 pounds. There are days that really get to me because like everyone else on this big blue marble we call earth, I have drama. Some of which I have caused, due to not making smart decisions, and others I have endured because of my loved ones. No matter how much I tell other women to learn to love and believe in themselves, I fall short and do not heed my own words. I am a very passionate person when it comes to self-esteem issues. As far as trusting men, I question a man's sexuality even if he just wears an earring. I have been labeled homophobic by some people. I try to explain that it is not about the homosexuality, but the deceit and selfishness of a down-low man. He is lying to everyone, including himself. He thinks it is okay to have sex with another man and then go home and make "love" to his mate.

At the present I am not dating—not due to bitterness—but because I am just being very cautious. If and when I do get married again, it will be because I have prayed to the True God and given him all the prerequisites I want in a mate. I am no longer just asking him to "please send me a man." I am currently working on promoting my book, *I Refuse To Be Lonely*, which at present I can hardly give away, but I am still proud of my work.

"Love at First Sight"

Nadine & Gerome

As far as Gerome is concerned, it has been 14 years since my discovery of his homosexuality. I just learned to deal with it because of our son. Our son is the link between us. We are really good friends, I must say. He helps me when I need it. He is a pretty good father—a lot better than he was. I have moved on with my life and have learned that I need to look deeper into a person before I say those infamous three words. That's all I can say.

"Desperately In Denial"

Keisha & Anthony

Believe it or not, I am still in my marriage with Anthony, even though I feel like I am in it all by myself. I know I am settling, but I don't want to be "just another" single mother without a husband. I am not happy, but I just can't bring myself to get a divorce, because I believe marriage is forever. I still pray to God about staying in my marriage, even though the pastor's wife told me a long time ago that according to scripture, I was free to leave. Do I love him? No!!!! Is it the money? No, because he has none of that. Is it the sex? No, because we hardly ever sleep together. To be honest, I really don't know why I am remaining in this marriage.

A month ago, my teenage daughter found more gay porn on our computer and I actually told her I didn't believe her. My daughter doesn't like her stepfather, Anthony, and she is very disappointed that I am still in this marriage. She tells me I can do so much better. I didn't know how to respond, I guess I am just afraid to leave.

In Conclusion

Straight Up

J.L. King's revelation that there was a secret behavior, known among men as the down-low, finally put a face on this life-threatening, deceitful, and cowardly behavior. We may not understand it, now or ever, but we must put up our line of defense and it starts with awareness. We need each other, ladies. This behavior is not destructive to one of us; it is destructive to all women regardless of race, creed, or color.

Since starting this book, we have spoken to *many* women who are going through this devastating experience. So please, ladies, don't think this can't happen to you and that it is a rare occurrence. According to the *Straight Spouse Network (SSN)*, it is estimated that up to two million gay individuals have married or will marry. We are not advocating that you live your life in fear, but we are encouraging you to use your own God-given common sense and be responsible for your own life. There is a common, somewhat demoralizing attitude that women are so desperate to have a man that they will take any man—no questions asked. That couldn't be farther from the truth. Since when did it become unnatural for a human being to want to experience romantic love. The three types of love are agape (God-like love), phileo (friendship-type love) and eros (romantic or erotic love). The point here is that the eros love is a part of our human nature, so to label women as "desperate" is demeaning and a very narcissistic way of thinking. Women are not looking to be deceived or lied to. They are being who God made them to be: loving, caring, nurturing human beings.

Men who are on the down-low choose to place the responsibility for their actions anywhere but on themselves. They even blame their culture or communities, especially the Black community, implying that the Black community is so archaic in its thinking that gay people must lie and deceive others and even marry in order to be accepted. They blame the Black church, yet gay men are commonly found directing the music department of many Black churches. They even blame their women for their homosexual urges. J. L. King, in his book *On The Down Low, A Journey Into the Lives of "Straight" Black Men Who Sleep With Men*, sums up the blame game as follows:

"I know quite a few down-low brothers (including the old me, before I came clean and started being honest with the people in my life) who have tried to convince a woman that it is her fault. These men will talk her into believing that she actually had something to do with their fooling around with men.

I recently had a conversation with a brother who had been married for seven years. When I asked him why he has unprotected sex with a man, he replied, "I trust this man. My wife has been getting on my nerves." He said that when he is with men, it's stress-free. No expectations. No lovemaking. Just sex.

His was a typical cop-out. She didn't drive him to do what he was doing. "Is she making you put your life at risk? Is she making you put her life at risk?" I asked. He just sat there and looked straight ahead. He didn't have an answer. He was satisfied in deflecting the guilt and blame away from himself.

J.L. King further stated...

"The bottom line is that I slept with men because that's what I liked—the same as all my down-low brothers."

In anonymous conversations on the Internet with down-low men, there was one thing the majority of them expressed and that was that they would never, ever tell their wives/girlfriends about their down-low lives. Their attitudes were, "What she doesn't know won't hurt her." One said "I will take this secret to the grave." This is the typical attitude of down-low men, which is why we women have to be supportive of each other. Unfortunately, history has shown us that women are divided rather than united during times of crisis.

After Terry McMillan appeared on Oprah with her estranged gay husband, a lot of the Internet message boards criticized her and made fun of her. African-American message boards were filled with comments from other women saying, "She should've known. Look at him. He looks gay. I would have known." They called her stupid and naïve among other things. First of all, a down-low man does not look gay when he is still undercover. He looks like the most eligible bachelor in the world to the woman in his sights. Terry McMillan's husband looked so much more gay on Oprah than when we originally saw him in print. Once he came out, he came out in his appearance also and definitely the world could see that he was gay, not because we are so much smarter than Terry, but because he was ready for us to see that he is gay. We believe that once the man comes out, his persona reflects his true nature. Some men become extremely promiscuous while others move in with their gay lovers.

Ladies, please understand that women who go through this need love, support and encouragement from their families and other women. When a woman catches her husband cheating with another woman, we automatically commiserate with her and provide her the necessary support. Women that have been taken through the down-low experience need our support just as much, if not more. They need a sister and a friend, not a critic. They have been deceived and betrayed. To be laughed at by other women is really another kind of betrayal. We call ourselves, "sisters," but from most of what we have experienced that is not what we really are to each other, and that includes all women, not just women of color. This non-supportive attitude is very prevalent in our society today and is perpetuated by men who enjoy the "cat-fights." We have to realize that if we don't respect other women, we don't respect ourselves because we are a reflection of one another. When we look in the faces of other women, we are looking at someone who is more like ourselves than not.

We need to take heed to all that is written in this book and other books on the subject of the down-low. It is not a myth, phase, phenomenon, fad or a product of media hype, as some would want us to believe. We shared our personal stories because we want society to hear and understand the profound effect this selfish lifestyle has on entire families. Many women did not include the devastation felt by their children in order to protect their anonymity. Some people believe in keeping secrets about almost anything. This is one secret nobody needs to keep. It is imperative that we continue to discuss this issue and educate ourselves. Even the gay community is adverse to the deceitfulness of down-low men. We interviewed an openly gay man who stated the following:

> *"It particularly angers me how these men try to get the best of both worlds. They want the status of being heterosexual, but then have sex with other men on the side. I think this is despicable. In the end, it just creates a lot of pain for all parties involved. I also wish gay men would not have sex with married men. It would force more married gay men to admit who they really are and would spare everyone a lot of pain.*
>
> *If I knew a woman married to a closeted gay man I'd tell her—if they were childless—to not have any kids with this guy and to dump him."*

The vaccination for polio was never needed until polio ravaged mankind and crippled people important to us. The vaccination did not become a cure. It was even better than that—it became a bonafide line of defense against a crippling disease. The down-low has been around since the beginning of time; however, we were unaware of its crippling effects, namely HIV/AIDS. We hope this book will aid in arming women with knowledge that will empower them with the tools to protect themselves.

The scientific and health-conscious community tells us that this down-low thing is such a phenomenon and that they have so many more studies to do. They reluctantly throw a statistic or two at us to let us think they really do care and are watching out for us, but they just can't give us any concrete numbers yet about the role the down-low plays in our escalating HIV rate. We want you to know it's much more than that. One lady who had been married to a down-low man for over 30 years gave a voice to all women devastated by down-low men.

"One night after watching a very handsome man singing a soft, sensual love song to his woman in a video, I realized tears were flowing down my cheeks like rain on a windshield. I hadn't even felt the cramp that must have happened in my heart in order for me to cry so freely. It was years ago that I found out about Melvin (not his real name), and still the loss of what he stole from me had a tight grip on my heart and mind. I went to my desk and wrote the following letter to Melvin. I didn't send the letter, but it had an affect on me akin to the eruption of a volcano that was asleep—but asleep only for a while."

Melvin:

Please read it all, until you have read every last word. Please. Because now that I realize who you were all this time, I can see now what I couldn't see before.

I heard a beautiful love song tonight. A man pouring out his heart to the woman he adored. This is the kind of love I deserved, the kind of man I deserved. Let my heart open up once and for all. I have been so deprived of the love I deserved. When I think of the men that begged me to just think about them, my heart breaks and breaks and breaks and sometimes tears run down my face no matter what I do. God, help me. This feeling of being cheated before I even knew what love could be... it hurts so bad. I know a man, some man... any other man would have loved me so much. I was soft, and warm, and loving, and I bore three beautiful children. When I began to grow old, those other men would have loved me and been turned on by me even more. I think of the men that told me I was pretty; the men that said they never thought someone like me would give them a chance; and then I think again, and again, and again... about how I never heard those words in my world. They were not for me. I was nothing. I felt like nothing. No matter what a good person, mother, and wife I tried to be... I was nothing. I was never fine. I was never soft. I was never special... and I was never beautiful... not to you.

Those words in that song are not from me to you. They are the words I yearn for. The words you never said to me because you couldn't say them to me. They are the words no one ever got a chance to say to me because you kept me as your hostage to watch you walk out of the door in your daisy dukes and tell me you were going to the barracks. They are the words a man would have said to me because he adored me... and knew I was something special. He would have said those words to me as he lovingly, gently caressed my face and looked into my eyes and showed me the tenderness you never did... because you never could. I don't blame you for being who you are, but why did you deceive me? Why didn't you just tell me that you preferred Ronald Barey, Big Eyed Greene, the tall big booty man that lived next door, George Word... yeah... George Word, and so many, many, more. I see their faces every day of my life... every day. I don't know most of their names anymore, but their faces I will never forget... even the tall, skinny, White man that came to our door one Sunday afternoon—lying—saying he sold vacuum cleaners. You knew each other... and don't let me forget Eugene. You acted as his mentor and I believed you were, but I was wrong. If I could, I would go to Fitzsimmons' job... I would stand outside and I would wait for him, your favorite lover of them all, the one you took showers with at your office. The one that shared your cubicle in your office. The one you invited over with his wife and you wore *your shorty robe for, the one you had me—your wife—beg for his marriage, while all the while you were doing him and he was doing you… the great Fitzsimmons. The one you went "hiking and shark fishing with." The one you lived with. Good old George Word… You dumped me out of a chair onto the floor for him. I was in your space that day. You told me Barey's wife put him out, but I wonder if he ever had a wife. You had your lover living in my house with me and your kids. Oh God. Oh God! What about the women you made me hate, because you told me they liked you just so you could throw me off the scent of the man in your sights. I pray God has mercy on you for what you've done to me. You used to go back and tell your lovers everything I said about them… just like a little bitch would do. No man does that to his wife. He would never betray his own wife for some dude. But you were a woman just like me. Why didn't you just tell me? I could have had a wonderful life. But, you chose to destroy my life because you were too much of a coward to live your own truth. I am going to get my life back and God is going to give me that wonderful lover of my soul that I always deserved… and I know it won't be long. In the mean-time, I wish you no ill feelings, but I know no good things will ever come your way until you say you are sorry for what you've done to me.*

May God have mercy on your soul.

ORDER FORM

Mail Checks or money orders payable to:

Creative Wisdom Books
P.O. Box 1154
Manassas, VA 20108

Please send ____ copy(ies) of *The Straight Up Truth About the Down-Low* to:

Name: _____

Address: _____

City: _____ State: _____ Zip: _____

Telephone: (____)_____/ (____)_____

Email: _____

I have enclosed $16.95, plus $4.00 shipping per book for a total of $_____.

Sales Tax: Add 5% to total cost of books for orders shipped to VA addresses.

For Bulk or Wholesale Rates, Call: 1-703-330-1996
Or email: CreativeWBooks@aol.com

For additional information, resources and support, please visit our website at www.straightuptruth.com